HOW TO PASS

THE POLICE SELECTION SYSTEM

WITHDRAWN

HOW TO PASS

THE POLICE SELECTION SYSTEM

Practise for the psychometric tests
and succeed at the assessment centres

3rd edition

HARRY TOLLEY,
BILLY HODGE &
CATHERINE TOLLEY

KoganPage

Publisher's note

Every possible effort has been made to ensure that the information contained in this book is accurate at the time of going to press, and the publishers and authors cannot accept responsibility for any errors or omissions, however caused. No responsibility for loss or damage occasioned to any person acting, or refraining from action, as a result of the material in this publication can be accepted by the editor, the publisher or any of the authors.

First published in Great Britain in 1997 entitled *How to Pass the Police Initial Recruitment Test*
Second edition published in 2004 entitled *How to Pass the New Police Selection System*
Revised second edition 2007
Third edition published in 2010 entitled *How to Pass the Police Selection System*

Kogan Page Limited
120 Pentonville Road
London N1 9JN
United Kingdom
www.koganpage.com

© Harry Tolley, Billy Hodge and Catherine Tolley, 1997, 2004, 2007, 2010

ISBN   978 0 7494 5712 9
E-ISBN 978 0 7494 5905 5

British Library Cataloguing in Publication Data

A CIP record for this book is available from the British Library.

Typeset by Saxon Graphics Ltd, Derby
Printed and bound in India by Replika Press Pvt Ltd

Contents

Becoming a police officer

Introduction

The **aim** of this chapter is to give you an overview of the **national selection system** by which police officers are now recruited to forces in England and Wales. Precise details of the procedures used at different stages in the process, and guidance on how you can prepare for them, are given in later chapters.

At present, although there is a national selection system for appointment as a police constable, there is no national police service. Instead, in addition to the British Transport Police and the Civil Nuclear Constabulary, there are 43 separate police forces covering England and Wales, 8 in Scotland and 1 in Northern Ireland – each force being run under the command of a Chief Officer. Although each force recruits independently, it does so within the framework provided by a national selection system. As a consequence, there is now a common set of entry requirements, at the heart of which are seven core competencies, which are judged to be relevant to the role of all police officers. A national assessment system has been established to ensure that all new entrants to the police service meet these selection criteria.

The following summary provides only general guidance on what you need to do, and what you can expect to experience should you decide to proceed with an application to become a police constable. As **Figure 1.1** shows, before you can be confirmed as a police officer you have to go through a series of stages at which assessments are made as to your suitability to proceed to the next stage. Even when you have been judged to have met all of the selection criteria at the end of the initial recruitment process you will still have to face two years of training, which will be rigorously supervised and assessed. Under the new **Initial Police Learning and Development Programme (IPLDP)** all new recruits are required to complete two years of locally delivered training, which on successful completion will lead to the award of a nationally recognized qualification in policing. However, the main purpose of this book is to provide you with guidance on the procedures used at different stages in the recruitment process (ie up to the point at which, if you are to be successful, your initial training or IPLDP will begin).

The national selection system

The first step you need to take in order to become a police officer is to check up on the information that is available online at www.policecouldyou.co.uk. Amongst other things, this website will tell you about the vacancy situation for the force(s) you wish to join and the waiting time before new applications can be processed – in some cases this may be as little as two to four weeks whereas in others it may be six months to a year. The website will also inform you about the recruitment and selection criteria that will be used to determine whether or not to proceed further with your application. At this initial stage the

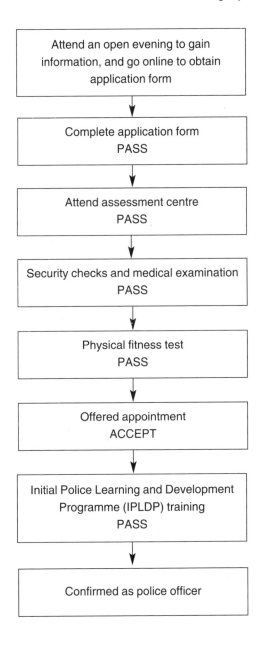

Figure 1.1 Becoming a police officer

recruiting department will be interested in whether or not you are eligible to apply, eg that you comply with the age limits and nationality requirements, and whether or not you have any criminal convictions or cautions for offences that would preclude your application being considered for appointment from the outset (see **Chapter 2**). It should be noted that, as an alternative to doing it in writing, you can complete the application form online via: www.policecouldyou.co.uk.

The completion of the **full application form** is a crucial part of the initial recruitment process – but don't be misled by the title. What you will receive is not a simple 'form', but a thick package that contains the following:

- information and instructions (4 pages);
- the application form (14 pages);
- questionnaires on equal opportunities and marketing (2 pages);
- information about the PE test (2 pages).

The information you are asked to provide in the questionnaires plays no part in the recruitment process, and to that end they will be detached from your application form on receipt.

As for the application form, you will find that it is divided into sections, which you must complete in person. In **Section 1** you are asked to provide the following information about yourself:

- personal details;
- forces to which you wish to apply;
- nationality;
- convictions and cautions – you are advised that you can obtain information on this matter on www.policecouldyou.co.uk or by calling at your nearest police recruitment office;
- health and eyesight;
- business interests;
- financial position;

- previous addresses;
- details about your family.

In **Section 2** of the application form you are asked to provide information about your present and previous employment and to give the names of two referees. There are two additional sub-sections, which have to be completed by: applicants who have served or are currently serving in HM Forces; those who have made previous applications to, or have a record of service with, a police force (eg as a police officer, Special Constable or support staff). **Section 3** then asks you to provide information about your education and skills, ie your education, qualifications and training, the skills you have acquired and any voluntary and community activities in which you are or have been involved.

If you are beginning to think that completing the application form is going to prove to be quite straightforward, you are in for a shock when you come to **Section 4**. It is at this point in the application form that you must begin to demonstrate that you have the core competencies you need if your application is to progress to the next stage in the recruitment process. In order to do that, you are asked to give written answers to 10 questions – four of which are divided into sub-sections. In each case you are expected to provide examples from your own experience and to write clear and concise answers, which may be up to 230 words in length. So you will need to pay attention to your handwriting, spelling and grammar as well as to the content of your answers – you are advised at the outset to answer truthfully as you may be asked to expand on your answers at a later stage. More precise details about the questions you will be asked, and guidance on how you can answer them, are given in **Chapter 7**.

After all that, you should find **Section 5** to be very straightforward. The first part is a declaration, which you have to sign to confirm that what you have said is true, that you have not withheld any relevant information and that you have read and understood a list of 10 statements. The second part is simply a checklist with boxes for you to tick, designed to ensure that you have completed all sections of the application form and included all of the necessary enclosures. You should now be in a position to send your completed application form to the recruitment office of your preferred police force – your application pack will include a list of addresses and contact details.

Assuming that the information you have provided is satisfactory, and that your answers to the questions you were asked are of the required standard, your name will be added to a waiting list for a place at an **assessment centre** – the next stage in the initial recruitment process. At the centre, when your turn arrives to attend, you will be required to complete four assessment tasks as follows: psychometric tests; report writing; role-play; and an interview. More precise details about what you should expect to experience at an assessment centre are given in **Chapter 3**.

The **psychometric tests** will be in two parts – a test of your number skills lasting 12 minutes in which you will be expected to answer 25 questions, and a verbal logical reasoning test in which you will have to answer 31 questions in 25 minutes. Further details about these two tests, guidance on how to prepare for them, and some practice tests for you to work through are given in **Chapters 4, 5 and 6**.

Your **writing** skills will be assessed by means of two writing exercises you will be asked to complete in a period of 40 minutes (ie 2 times 20 minutes). In each case you will be asked to respond to a complaint or an issue by writing a short report. The assessors will take into consideration the content of what you write as well as your handwriting, spelling, punctuation and grammar. Further details about this test and guidance on how to prepare for it are given in **Chapter 7**.

After the writing test, your oral communication and interpersonal skills will be assessed by means of four **role-play** activities – one after the other with no time for a break in between and each one lasting five minutes. For each activity you will be given a short written account of a situation (or 'scenario'), and a role to play when it is acted out between you and another person. That person will be someone who has been trained to play their part in such a way that you will be confronted with realistic problems similar to those that police officers encounter in the course of their duties. Your performance in dealing with the people, and the problems they present you with, will be observed closely and assessed – video recordings being used to monitor the standards of assessment. Further details about the role-play activities, and guidance on how to prepare for them, are given in **Chapter 8.**

Finally, you will be given a **structured interview** lasting 20 minutes during which you will be asked to answer four questions as well as deal with any matters arising from the contents of your application form. Further information about the interview, including guidance on how to prepare for it, is given in **Chapter 9.**

You should not expect to receive any immediate feedback on how you performed at the assessment centre – all you can expect is a well-earned cup of tea or coffee before you leave! You will be assessed and graded A–D on each of the four activities – a grade D for any one of them resulting in failure, and your elimination for the time being at least from the initial recruitment process. In the case of the crucial 'respect for diversity' criterion, a grade D will result in a six-month wait at least. However, if you have succeeded in reaching the required standard on all four of the assessments you should receive a letter to that effect within 10 days. You will then be subjected to **security checks** and required to undergo a **medical examination.** Once you have negotiated those two hurdles you will have to prove your physical fitness, which will be assessed by a standard **PE test**, further details of which are given in **Chapter 10.** Candidates who failed at the assessment centre stage must wait for six months before they can reapply.

The PE test marks the end of the initial recruitment process. If you have succeeded in meeting the required standards at each stage you will be called in to the recruitment office of your preferred force and offered an appointment. If you accept, you will then start on your **IPLDP training**, the satisfactory completion of which will qualify you to become a police officer.

Unfortunately, many would-be entrants to the police service will be unsuccessful, because at some point in the assessment system described above they will fail to demonstrate their true potential. Failure may be the result of a variety of factors, including: anxiety and stress; having to complete psychometric tests quickly and accurately under test conditions; having to perform in front of other people whilst being observed and evaluated; and not knowing what skills and abilities are being assessed. However, careful and systematic preparation for the whole initial recruitment process, using the information, guidance and practice tests provided in this book, can help to overcome the causes of failure listed above – and in so doing avoid the sense of disappointment and frustrated ambition which inevitably follows.

The purpose of this book, therefore, is to offer guidance to would-be police officers on how to prepare themselves for the initial recruitment process, and in particular for the types of assessment, which they will encounter at different stages in the national selection system. We begin in **Chapter 2** by looking at the official entry requirements, which they must satisfy, and at the competencies that recruiters are required to look for in future police officers.

2

Entry requirements and competencies

The **aim** of this chapter is to give you guidance on the entry requirements for the police service and the competencies – at this stage think of them as a mixture of attitudes, skills, abilities and personal attributes – you will need if you are to become a police officer. This should help to give you a better understanding of the qualities you will be expected to display at different stages in the initial recruitment process as described in **Chapter 1**.

Entry requirements

As part of the official procedures, it is necessary for police forces to proceed only with those applicants who meet the recruitment and selection criteria. So, simply to be eligible for entry to the police service you must:

■ Be at least 18 years of age before you can be appointed. There is no upper age limit, although the normal retirement age for constables is currently 55 years of age and there is a two-year probationary period to be completed.

■ Be a British citizen, a member of the EC/EEA, Commonwealth or other country and have been resident in the United Kingdom (UK) for three or more years, with unrestricted permission to remain in the UK.

■ Declare if you are a serving member of HM Forces and be within six months of a confirmed discharge date.

■ Meet the required eyesight standards. Using the Snellen's Test an acceptable standard for unaided vision is no less than 6/36 in each eye and for aided vision 6/12 in either eye and 6/6 binocularly. (If in doubt, check with your optician.)

■ Declare if you have been convicted or cautioned of an offence (including traffic convictions, appearances before a court martial and 'spent' convictions applicable under the Rehabilitation of Offenders Act 1974) at any time. You may still be eligible for appointment depending on the nature and circumstances of the offence. (As indicated in **Chapter 1** you will be asked to give details on an initial self-assessment form.)

■ Not be in the process of applying to another force.

■ Be physically fit enough to perform the duties of a constable, and safely and effectively handle police equipment. This will be tested during the initial recruitment process.

■ Be in good health mentally and physically to undertake police duties. Police officers encounter stressful situations, trauma, physical confrontation and work long hours and shifts.

Competencies relevant to the role of a police officer

The **Could You?** brochure, which is issued to those seeking a career as a police officer, illustrates just how demanding the role has become. For example, the booklet asks you to consider whether or not you could 'tell a child that his parents have been killed by a drunken driver', 'help your police colleagues to break down a door on a drugs raid', stay calm if people started 'shouting racial abuse at you', and 'arrest an old woman caught stealing food in the supermarket because she could not afford to eat'? So, before you proceed any further with your application, it would be sensible for you to think hard, not just about how you would handle situations like these, but also about how they might affect you as a person.

The above examples have been deliberately chosen to provoke that kind of reflection on the part of would-be applicants to the police service. As such, they provide a stark reminder that the day-to-day work of modern police officers requires physical, mental and moral courage, combined with intelligence, good communication skills, flexibility, a strong sense of values and sensitivity to the thoughts, feelings and beliefs of others. These personal qualities have now been made explicit as a set of seven 'competencies relevant to the role of a police constable'. These competencies have then been used to inform the design of the national selection system described in **Chapter 1**, and to define the aims of foundation and probationer training.

So, if you are still interested in becoming a police officer, it's worth spending a little time becoming more familiar with them. The competencies have been defined under the headings given below:

- community and customer focus;
- effective communication;
- personal responsibility;
- problem solving;
- resilience;
- respect for race and diversity;
- team working.

As you will see in the lists given below, these competencies have then been broken down into descriptions of actions and behaviours, which enable assessors to establish whether or not a person possesses them to the 'required standard'. In addition, 'negative indicators' have been identified which, if someone displays them, will be taken as a signal that the person definitely lacks the necessary competence.

A good starting point in your preparation for the selection process, therefore, would be to use the information provided below to carry out a self-assessment of how you 'measure up' against each of the competencies. This should serve two useful purposes. First, it will help you to become familiar with the competencies, and the way in which they have been articulated. Second, it will provide you with a broad indication of your strengths and weaknesses in relation to the competencies, and the standards you will be expected to reach. You should then be in a position to build on those strengths, and to work on your weaknesses in order to improve your chances of success in the assessments you will face as part of the initial recruitment process.

Start by reading the numbered statements (including the 'negative indicators') and then try to decide how accurately each describes the way you normally act or behave – in other words, how competent you are. In each case, record your decision by placing a number alongside the statement where:

1   =   I always act or behave in this way
2   =   I sometimes act or behave in this way
3   =   I rarely/never act or behave in this way

Remember, this is not a task to be rushed, as you will need to give careful thought to each statement before reaching your decision, and to the evidence on which your judgement was based. Given that there are seven sets of statements for you to work through, it might be an idea, therefore, for you to break the task down into parts, rather than trying to complete it all at once. Finally, it would be sensible at some stage to crosscheck the outcomes of your self-assessment audit with someone who knows you well and whose judgements you can trust.

Community and customer focus

Police officers are expected to: focus on the customer and to provide a high quality service that is tailored to meet their individual needs; understand the communities that are being served; and to show an active commitment to policing that reflects their needs and concerns. In order to do this they must: provide a high level of service to customers; maintain contact with customers; work out what they need and respond to them.

Required standard

1. I present an appropriate image to the public and other organizations.
2. I support strategies that aim to build an organization that reflects the community it serves.
3. I focus on the customer in all activities.
4. I try to sort out customers' problems as quickly as possible.
5. I apologize when I am at fault or have made mistakes.
6. I respond quickly to customer requests.
7. I make sure that customers are satisfied with the service they receive.
8. I manage customer expectations.
9. I keep customers updated on progress.
10. I balance community and organizational interests.
11. I sort out errors or mistakes as quickly as possible.

Negative indicators

1. I am not customer-focused and do not consider individual needs.
2. I do not tell customers what is going on.
3. I present an unprofessional image to customers.
4. I only see a situation from my own view, not from the customer's view.

5. I show little interest in the customer and only deal with their immediate problem.
6. I do not respond to the needs of the local community.
7. I am slow to respond to customers' requests.
8. I fail to check that customers' needs have been met.
9. I focus on organizational issues rather than customer needs.
10. I do not make the most out of opportunities to talk to people in the community.

Effective communication

Police officers must be able to: communicate ideas and information effectively, both verbally and in writing; use language and a style of communication that is appropriate to the situation and the people being addressed; and, make sure that others understand what is going on. In order to do this they must: communicate all needs, instructions and decisions clearly; adapt the style of communication to meet the needs of the audience; and check for understanding.

Required standard
1. I deal with issues directly.
2. I clearly communicate needs and instructions.
3. I clearly explain management decisions and policy, and the reasons behind them.
4. I communicate face to face wherever possible and if it is appropriate.
5. I speak with authority and confidence.
6. I change the style of communication to meet the needs of the audience.
7. I manage group discussions effectively.
8. I summarize information to check people understand it.
9. I support arguments and recommendations effectively in writing.
10. I produce well-structured reports and written summaries.

Negative indicators
1. I am hesitant, nervous and uncertain when speaking.
2. I speak without first thinking through what to say.
3. I use inappropriate language or jargon.
4. I speak in a rambling way.
5. I do not consider the target audience.
6. I avoid answering difficult questions.
7. I do not give full information without being questioned.
8. I write in an unstructured way.
9. I use poor spelling, punctuation and grammar.
10. I assume that others understand what has been said without actually checking.
11. I do not listen, and interrupt at inappropriate times.

Personal responsibility

Police officers are expected to: take personal responsibility for making things happen and achieving results; display motivation, commitment, perseverance, and conscientiousness; and, act with a high degree of integrity. In order to do this they must: take responsibility for their own actions; sort out issues or problems as they arise; focus on achieving results to the required standards; and, develop their skills and knowledge.

Required standard
1. I accept personal responsibility for my own actions.
2. I display initiative, taking on tasks without having to be asked.
3. I take action to resolve problems and fulfil my own responsibilities.
4. I keep promises and do not let colleagues down.
5. I take pride in my own work.
6. I am conscientious in completing work on time.
7. I follow things through to a satisfactory conclusion.

8. I am self-motivated, showing enthusiasm and dedication to my role.
9. I focus on a task even if it is routine.
10. I improve my own job-related knowledge and keep it up-to-date.
11. I am open, honest and genuine, standing up for what is right.
12. I make decisions based upon ethical considerations and organizational integrity.
13. I am aware of my own strengths and weaknesses.

Negative indicators

1. I pass responsibility upwards inappropriately.
2. I am not concerned about letting others down.
3. I will not deal with issues – I just hope that they will go away.
4. I blame others rather than admitting to mistakes or looking for help.
5. I am unwilling to take on responsibility.
6. I put in the minimum effort that is needed to get by.
7. I show a negative and disruptive attitude.
8. I show little energy or enthusiasm for work.
9. I express a cynical attitude to the organization and the job.
10. I give up easily when faced with problems.
11. I fail to recognize my personal weaknesses and development needs.
12. I make little or no attempt to develop myself or to keep up-to-date.

Problem solving

Police officers must be able to: gather information from a range of sources; analyse information to identify problems and issues; and, make effective decisions. In order to do this they must: gather enough relevant information to understand specific issues and events; use information to identify problems and draw logical conclusions; and, make good decisions.

Required standard

1. I identify where to get information and get it.
2. I get as much information as is appropriate on all aspects of a problem.
3. I separate relevant information from irrelevant information, and important information from unimportant information.
4. I take in information quickly and accurately.
5. I review all the information gathered to understand the situation and draw logical conclusions.
6. I identify and link causes and effects.
7. I identify what can and cannot be changed.
8. I take a systematic approach to solving problems.
9. I remain impartial and avoid jumping to conclusions.
10. I refer to procedures and precedents as necessary, before making decisions.
11. I make good decisions that take account of all relevant factors.

Negative indicators

1. I do not deal with problems in detail and do not identify underlying issues.
2. I do not gather enough information before coming to conclusions.
3. I do not consult other people who may have extra information.
4. I do not research the background to problems.
5. I show no interest in gathering or using intelligence.
6. I do not gather evidence.
7. I make assumptions about the facts of a situation.
8. I do not notice problems until they have become significant issues.

9. I get stuck in the detail of complex situations and cannot see the main issues.
10. I react without considering all the angles.
11. I become distracted by minor issues.

Resilience

Police officers are required to: show resilience, even in difficult circumstances; be prepared to make difficult decisions; and, have the confidence to see them through. In order to do this they must: show reliability and resilience in difficult circumstances; remain calm and confident; and, respond logically and decisively in difficult situations.

Required standard

1. I am reliable in a crisis, remain calm and think clearly.
2. I sort out conflict and deal with hostility and provocation in a calm and restrained way.
3. I respond to challenges rationally, avoiding inappropriate emotion.
4. I deal with difficult emotional issues and then move on.
5. I manage conflicting pressures and tensions.
6. I maintain professional ethics when confronted with pressure from others.
7. I cope with ambiguity and deal with uncertainty and frustration.
8. I resist pressure to make quick decisions where full consideration is needed.
9. I remain focused and in control of situations.
10. I make and carry through decisions, even if they are unpopular, difficult or controversial.
11. I stand firmly by a position when it is right to do so.
12. I defend my colleagues from excessive criticism from outside the team.

Negative indicators

1. I get easily upset, frustrated and annoyed.
2. I panic and become agitated when problems arise.
3. I walk away from confrontation when it would be more appropriate to get involved.
4. I need constant reassurance, support and supervision.
5. I use inappropriate physical force.
6. I get too emotionally involved in situations.
7. I react inappropriately when faced with rude or abusive people.
8. I deal with situations aggressively.
9. I complain and whinge about problems rather than dealing with them.
10. I give in inappropriately when under pressure.
11. I worry about making mistakes and avoid difficult situations whenever possible.

Respect for race and diversity

Police officers are required to consider and show respect for the opinions, circumstances and feelings of colleagues, and members of the public, no matter what their race, religion, position, background, circumstances, status or appearance. In order to do this they must: understand other people's views and take them into account; be tactful and diplomatic when dealing with people, treating them with dignity and respect at all times; and, understand and be sensitive to social, cultural and racial differences.

Required standard

1. I see issues from other people's viewpoints.
2. I am polite, tolerant and patient when dealing with people, treating them with respect and dignity.
3. I respect the needs of everyone involved when sorting out disagreements.

4. I show understanding and sensitivity to people's problems and vulnerabilities.
5. I deal with diversity issues and give positive practical support to colleagues who may feel vulnerable.
6. I listen to and value other's views and opinions.
7. I use language in an appropriate way and I am sensitive to the way it may affect people.
8. I acknowledge and respect a broad range of social and cultural customs, beliefs and values within the law.
9. I understand what offends others and adapt my own actions accordingly.
10. I respect and maintain confidentiality, wherever appropriate.
11. I deliver difficult messages sensitively.
12. I challenge inappropriate attitudes, language and behaviour that is abusive, aggressive or discriminatory.
13. I take into account personal needs and interests of others.
14. I support minority groups both inside and outside the organization.

Negative indicators
1. I do not consider other people's feelings.
2. I do not encourage people to talk about personal issues.
3. I criticize people without considering their feelings and motivation.
4. I make situations worse with inappropriate remarks, language or behaviour.
5. I am thoughtless and tactless when dealing with people.
6. I am dismissive and impatient with people.
7. I do not respect confidentiality.
8. I unnecessarily emphasize power and control in situations where this is not appropriate.
9. I intimidate others in an aggressive and overpowering way.
10. I use humour inappropriately.
11. I show bias and prejudice when dealing with people.

Team working

Police officers must: develop strong working relationships inside and outside the team to achieve common goals; break down barriers between groups; and, involve others in discussions and in making decisions. In order to do this they must: work effectively as a team member and help build relationships within it; and, actively help and support others to achieve team goals.

Required standard
1. I understand my own role in a team.
2. I actively support and assist others in the team to achieve their objectives.
3. I am approachable and friendly to others.
4. I make time to get to know people.
5. I cooperate with and support others.
6. I offer to help other people.
7. I ask for and accept help when needed.
8. I develop mutual trust and confidence in others.
9. I willingly take on unpopular or routine tasks.
10. I contribute to team objectives no matter what the direct personal benefit may be.
11. I acknowledge that there is often a need to be a member of more than one team.
12. I take pride in my team and promote its performance to others.

Negative indicators
1. I do not volunteer to help other team members.
2. I am only interested in taking part in high profile and interesting activities.
3. I take credit for successes without recognizing the contribution of others.
4. I work to my own agenda rather than contributing to team performance.

5. I allow small exclusive groups of people to develop.
6. I play one person off against another.
7. I restrict and control what information is shared.
8. I do not let people say what they think.
9. I do not offer advice or get advice from others.
10. I show little interest in working jointly with other groups to meet the goals of everyone involved.
11. I do not discourage conflict within the organization.

When you have finished your self-assessments you should ask yourself the following questions:

- What do the completed patterns of responses tell you about yourself?
- What are the strengths on which you can build?
- What are the weaknesses, which you need to address?

When looking at your responses, remember that a number **1** against a 'required standard' statement indicates strength – because you have decided that you always act and behave in that way. However, when looking at your responses to the 'negative indicator' statements it is a number **3** which indicates strength – because in this case you have decided that you rarely/never act or behave in that way. It should be noted that with weaknesses the reverse is the case.

When you have done that analysis, you might consider drawing up an **action plan** aimed at furthering your personal development using the guidance offered elsewhere in this book. To that end, you could begin by making yourself a series of boxes (one for each core competency) based on the example given below.

Respect for race and diversity

I need to work on the following aspects of respecting diversity (arranged in order of importance):

I intend to do this by (list the **actions** you intend to take in order to improve in relation to this competency):

Note: The importance of this competency cannot be overstated. It is assessed in everything except the psychometric tests – a low grade in it leading to automatic failure.

Coming on top of the entry requirements and competencies outlined above, the prospect of facing the different assessment tests, which make up the initial recruitment system, probably seems quite daunting. It is important to remember, therefore, that the selection process is not intended to be easy. Those responsible for designing it know from experience that if someone fails to meet the required standard on the assessment tasks that have been set, it is unlikely that they will cope with the demands of foundation and probation training. They have a responsibility, which they take very seriously, to select, from the large number of applications they receive, those candidates whom they judge to have a good chance of becoming effective and successful police officers. If you think that you measure up to those exacting standards you will now be ready for the guidance offered in **Chapter 3**.

3

The assessment centre

If you are eligible to apply for entry to the police service, and the contents of your application form are satisfactory, you will be invited to attend an assessment centre. The time you are there will be used to obtain further information about your suitability for recruitment as a police officer. The **aim** of this chapter, therefore, is to provide you with information about the assessment centre in order to help you to prepare for that experience. It is designed to lead you into the subsequent chapters of the book, which will provide you with additional guidance on the assessment tasks you will be asked to undertake at the centre.

What is an assessment centre?

The term 'assessment centre' really describes a process and not a place. Typically, that process involves the close observation of participants whilst they take part in a series of activities – many of which involve their interactions with each other. These exercises have been designed to enable an assessment to be made of the potential future job performance of those invited to participate. To that end, each candidate is assessed against a set of criteria, which have been derived from an analysis of the competencies relevant to a particular job. Consequently, the following procedures are used at an assessment centre:

- Assessments are made on the basis of what the candidates do and how they do it.
- Trained assessors evaluate the performance of each candidate in activities, using criteria derived from the relevant competencies (**Chapter 2**).
- Data collected from all of the activities are used to determine the final result.

You can find out more about assessment centres by reading *How to Succeed at an Assessment Centre, 3rd edition* (Tolley and Wood), a book in this series, published by Kogan Page.

Timetable

When you get there you will find that the assessment centre follows a strict timetable in order to administer a morning and afternoon session. So, when you are told that you must arrive by a certain time you should do everything in your power to be punctual. Candidates who arrive late will not be allowed to participate in the proceedings on that occasion. Attendance at an alternative assessment centre, later that day or during that week may be permitted, but only in exceptional circumstances. Otherwise you will be referred back to the police force through which you made your application.

The assessments will be undertaken over a period lasting approximately **3 hours 30 minutes**. When you arrive you will be asked to complete a registration form. After an ID check you will be issued with a six digit number, which you will be asked to wear at all times. You will then be given a **preliminary briefing** – an initial overview – about what will happen, followed by an opportunity to ask questions and resolve any related difficulties. You will then be ready to proceed with the assessment exercises, each of which will be preceded by a full briefing.

Assessment exercises

Your performance will be assessed on each of the following:

- two psychometric tests – one to assess your number skills and the other verbal logical reasoning;
- two written exercises;
- four role-play exercises;
- a structured interview.

All of the candidates will undertake the same exercises and you will be assessed on a fair and equal basis using the same criteria.

In both the written and the role-play exercises, you will be asked to assume the role of a Customer Services Officer who has recently been appointed at a retail and leisure complex. For the purposes of the exercises this has been given a fictitious name – 'The Westshire Centre'. You will be given details of your duties and responsibilities together with information about the complex in the form of a 'Welcome Pack'. You *must* take advantage of every opportunity to familiarize yourself with its contents. Figure 3.1 summarizes your situation with regard to the written and role-play exercises.

Psychometric tests

The psychometric tests will be in two parts. First, you will be given a test of your **number skills** lasting 12 minutes in which you will be expected to answer 25 multiple choice questions. In each case you will be given a short number problem and five possible answers, A to E, only one of which is correct. You have to decide which one it is. Second, you will be given a test of your **verbal logical reasoning** skills in which you will be asked to answer 31 questions in 25 minutes. In each question you will be given a description of an imaginary event, together with additional facts which are known about it. This is then followed by

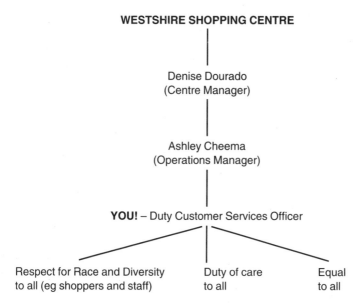

WESTSHIRE SHOPPING CENTRE

Denise Dourado
(Centre Manager)

Ashley Cheema
(Operations Manager)

YOU! – Duty Customer Services Officer

Respect for Race and Diversity
to all (eg shoppers and staff)

Duty of care
to all

Equal
to all

Figure 3.1 The Westshire Shopping Centre

a list of conclusions, which might be derived from the information provided. You have to evaluate each of the conclusions given, and then, in the light of the evidence, decide if it is 'true', 'false' or 'impossible to say'. Further details about these two tests, guidance on how to prepare for them, and some examples for you to practise on are given in **Chapters 4, 5 and 6**.

Written exercises

The two written exercises will last for a total of 40 minutes – divided equally between them. You will be shown into a room along with the other candidates in your group where a trained assessor will brief you before you start each exercise. You will then be given additional instructions and be asked to provide written responses, eg to a letter of complaint from a customer or a matter raised by the centre's Operations Manager (see Figure

3.1). The precise details can be changed from time to time so you should be prepared to follow the instructions carefully in writing your reports.

Lined paper and pens will be provided. You will be allowed to make rough notes, which will not be assessed. You will be notified during both exercises when you have five minutes remaining, and then again when there is one minute left. What you write will not be assessed at the time, but after you have completed the assessment centre. Further guidance on the written exercises and how to prepare for them is given in **Chapter 7**.

Role-play exercises

Each of the four role-play exercises will be split into two five-minute parts: a preparation phase; and an interactive phase (or role-play). In the former, you will be provided with written information relevant to the exercise concerned. You will be allocated a space where you will have five minutes to study the information and prepare for the role-play phase. If you wish to make notes on the paper supplied you may do so and you may refer to them during the role-play itself. You will not be assessed on the work you do during the preparatory stage. A buzzer will sound after five minutes to signal that it is time for you to move to an activity room. Remember to take the material you have prepared with you.

In the next phase you will interact, in your given role (a newly appointed Customer Services Officer), with a trained actor. In each exercise the actor may be male or female, and the written information provided for use in the preparation phase will have taken this into account. You will be expected to take the initiative and the actor will respond using lines which will have been rehearsed beforehand. A trained assessor will be in the room to observe the interactions. That person will make a written assessment, at the same time, of what you do and how you do it. In addition, an independent observer may be present in the room.

The following is an overview of the four interactive exercises that you will be required to undertake. It should be noted that, for the purposes of the exercises, the people you meet will be given fictitious names:

- the Operations Manager, who seeks your ideas on how to deal with a centre issue;
- a customer, who wishes to see you regarding an interaction with a security guard;
- a customer, who wants to discuss the behaviour of youths in the centre;
- a worker in the centre, who wants to discuss an issue with you.

Further guidance on the role-play exercises and how to prepare for them is given in **Chapter 8**.

Interview

The interview will last for a maximum of 20 minutes in which you will be asked four questions about how you have dealt with specific situations in the past. You will be allowed up to five minutes to answer each question. As the interviewer asks you the question, you will also be given a copy to which you can refer. The interviewer may ask you further questions to probe your answers and to help you to provide a fuller response. During the interview you will be assessed on five competencies: respect for diversity; team working; personal responsibility; resilience; and effective communication. Further guidance on the interview and how to prepare for it is given in **Chapter 9**.

Conduct of the assessments

The assessment centre has been designed to ensure that each of the seven core competencies will be assessed on at least three occasions – respect for diversity being assessed in every exercise. Consequently, you should not be unduly concerned if you feel that you have not done well in any one exercise, as you will have at least two other exercises where the same competencies will be assessed again. Your performance in each competency area within an exercise will be awarded a grade on a scale from A to D. A is awarded to the highest-performing candidates and D to the least strongly performing candidates. Remember, you will be awarded a grade in relation to **what** you do and **how** you do it.

Other people will be present at the assessment centre process at the same time – though they may complete the separate stages in a different order to you. For example, one group may undertake the interviews first whilst another group may start with the written exercises. There will be a preliminary briefing on the day and the order in which you will undertake the exercises will be fully explained.

The majority of the assessors, role actors and interviewers will be either police officers or civilian staff from the police forces who are sending candidates to the assessment centre. They may also have been selected specifically from the community. All the assessors, actors and interviewers will be highly trained and **their** conduct and performance will be monitored throughout the assessment centre. They will work to a predetermined assessment guide; the only information they will have about you will be your candidate number, which will be allocated to you on arrival.

Finally, your results will be sent to the police organization which is dealing with your application for employment, and that organization will pass them on to you. Every effort will be made to do that as quickly as possible.

Final thoughts

It is in your best interests to report to the assessment centre punctually, smartly dressed and ready for any eventuality. You should be careful of your behaviour, the language you use and the attitudes you display throughout your time at the centre – you cannot afford to have moments when you are caught 'off guard'. That person with whom you had a chat over coffee and to whom you made some ill-considered remarks on a controversial subject may turn out to have been an assessor and not a fellow candidate. It is not unknown for applicants to be asked to leave an assessment centre early because of such indiscretions!

4

How to prepare for the psychometric tests

The **aims** of this chapter are to help you to: understand how practice can have a positive effect on the grades you achieve on the psychometric tests you will be required to take at the assessment centre; perform to the best of your ability under test conditions; and, make effective use of the practice tests provided in **Chapters 5** and **6** of this book, including how to interpret your scores.

How practice can make a difference

Many candidates underachieve in selection tests because they are overanxious and because they have not known what to expect. Practice tests are designed to help you to overcome both of these common causes of failure. The practice tests provided in this book will help you to become familiar with two of the tests you will be required to take at the assessment centre. Regular practice will also give you the opportunity to work under conditions similar to those you will experience when taking the real test. In particular, they should help you to become accustomed to working under the pressure of the strict time limits which are imposed in standardized tests. Familiarity with the demands of the tests and working under simulated test conditions should help you to cope better with any nervousness you might experience when the result really matters.

How to perform to the best of your ability

Our experience over many years of preparing candidates for public examinations and standardized tests leads us to suggest that if you want to perform to the best of your ability in a selection test like the ones used as part of the police initial recruitment process you should read and act on the advice given below:

- Make sure that you know what you have to do before you start putting pencil to paper – if you do not understand, ask the person who is administering the test.
- Read the instructions carefully before each test starts in order to make sure that you understand them. Don't skim through them – you may overlook important details and in consequence make mistakes you could have avoided.
- Even if you have taken the test before, don't assume that the instructions (and the worked examples) are the same as last time – they may have been changed.
- Read the instructions carefully and highlight/underline the 'command words' (ie those words that tell you what to do).
- Once the test begins, work as quickly and accurately as you can. Remember, every unanswered item is a scoring chance you have missed!
- Check frequently to make sure that the questions you have answered match the spaces you have filled in on the answer sheet – the right answer in the wrong place will be marked as incorrect!

- Avoid spending too much time on questions you find difficult – leave them and go back to them later if you have time to do so.
- If you are uncertain about an answer, enter your best-reasoned choice – but avoid simply 'guessing'.
- If you have time to spare after you have answered all the questions, go back and check through your answers.
- Keep on working as hard as you can throughout the test – the more correct answers you get the higher your score will be.
- Concentrate your mind on the test itself and nothing else – you cannot afford to allow yourself to be distracted.
- Try to be positive in your attitude. Previous failures in tests or examinations are in the past – don't allow them to have a detrimental effect on your performance on this occasion.

How to use the practice tests

In order to derive maximum benefit from the use of practice tests you should read and act on the advice given below. This consists of three sets of checklists to guide you through different stages, ie **before** you begin, **during** a practice test and **after** you have completed it.

Before you attempt any of the tests make sure that you:

- have a supply of sharpened pencils, an eraser and some paper for doing rough work;
- have a clock or watch with an alarm which you can set to make sure that you work within the recommended time limits;
- are in a quiet room where you will not be disturbed or distracted, and which has an uncluttered desk/table at which you can work;
- have decided in advance which test(s) you are going to tackle;

- have reviewed what you learnt from previous practice sessions;
- have read the instructions (given at the start of the relevant chapter) on how to complete the test, making sure that you understand them before you begin;
- have worked through the examples provided so that you know exactly what to do before you start;
- know how to record your answers correctly.

You should then be ready to set your timer and tackle the chosen practice test.

During the practice test itself you should try to:

- work quickly and systematically through all the items – and whatever you do, don't panic;
- move on to the next question as quickly as you can if you get stuck at any point – you can always return to the unfinished items at the end if you have time to do so;
- check your answers if you have time to do so at the end;
- use spare paper for your rough work;
- stop working as soon as the time is up (and mark the point you have reached in the test if there are any items which you have not yet completed).

After the practice test you should:

- check your answers by referring to the answers given at the end of the relevant chapter;
- put a (✓) against each question that you answered correctly and a (✗) next to each one you got wrong;
- only score as correct those questions in which you filled in exactly the right answer spaces – anything different from those given in the answer sheet should be marked incorrect;
- add up the number of ticks to give you your score on the test as a whole;
- compare your score with those on previous tests of the same type to see what progress you are making;

■ work through any items that you did not manage to complete in the test and check your answers;
■ try to work out where you went wrong with any questions that you answered incorrectly.

Try to talk through the methods you used to arrive at your answers with someone who has also completed the test. This will help to consolidate your learning by:

■ helping you to understand why you got the answer to certain questions wrong;
■ giving you a better understanding of the questions to which you got the correct answers;
■ suggesting different ways of arriving at the same answer to a question.

Discussion of this kind should also help you to reach an understanding of the principles that underpin the design and construction of a test. If you can begin to get 'inside the mind' of the person who set the questions you will be in a much better position to answer them when required to do so in a real test. This would be an especially useful way of preparing for the **verbal logical reasoning** test. Working collaboratively with another person can also help to keep you motivated and provide you with encouragement and 'moral' support if and when you need it.

Interpreting your practice test scores

Because they have not been taken under exactly the same conditions as the real tests you should not read too much into your practice test scores. You will probably find that the real tests will be more exacting because they will be administered formally in a standardized way by a person who has been trained in their use, and will be more stressful than practice tests.

Nevertheless, your practice test scores should provide you with some useful **feedback** on the following: how your performance on the same type of test (eg numerical reasoning) has varied from one practice test to another, and hence what progress you have made over a given period of time; how well you have done on one type of test compared to another, and hence what your relative strengths and weaknesses seem to be.

However, when trying to make sense of your practice test scores you should remember that the scores you achieve will be compared with the standards achieved by a group of typical candidates in order to determine how well or badly you have done.

Making use of feedback from practice tests

More important than your total score on a practice test is **how** you achieved that overall mark. For example, you could begin such an analysis by noting the answers to the following questions:

- How many questions did you attempt within the given time limit and how many remained unanswered?
- How many of the questions that you attempted did you answer correctly?
- Where in the practice test were most of your incorrect answers (eg at the end when you were hurrying, or at the beginning before you had calmed your nerves and settled down to work)?
- Were there any particular types of question that you got wrong?

The answers to these questions should give you some pointers as to how you might **improve** your scores in future practice tests by helping you to change your behaviour. For example:

■ If you got most of the questions right but left too many unanswered, you should try to work more quickly next time.

■ If you managed to answer all the questions but got a lot of them wrong, you should try to be more accurate even if this means that you have to work more slowly.

Remember, the object of the exercise in standardized tests is to score as many correct answers as you can in the time allowed. Thus, you need to strike a balance between speed and accuracy. Regular practice, careful evaluation of your performance and intelligent use of feedback can help you to get the right balance.

Other ways of preparing for the psychometric tests

Further practice tests, which are relevant to those used in the police initial recruitment process, are available in other books in this series. For example, if you are interested in further developing your **verbal logical reasoning skills** we recommend that you use *How to Pass Verbal Reasoning Tests*, 4th edition (Tolley and Thomas, published by Kogan Page). In addition to using the practice tests we suggest that you make use of the guidance offered in **Chapter 2** of that book on the other things that you can do to improve your verbal usage and reasoning skills. Similarly, if your aim is to improve your **numerical reasoning skills** we advise you to consult *How to Pass Numeracy Tests*, 4th edition (Tolley and Thomas, published by Kogan Page). Once again, in addition to examples of different types of number tests on which you can practise, suggestions are provided in **Chapter 2** for things you can do to develop your competence in numerical reasoning.

5

Numerical reasoning test

Introduction

This is a multiple-choice test, the aim of which is to test your skills in basic numeracy. To that end, you will be presented with a series of number problems for which you are required to choose the correct answers from a choice of five possible (A–E). You do **not** have to show how you arrived at your answer – you simply indicate your choice according to the instructions.

You are not allowed to use a calculator in the test, so you should try to work without one whenever you can. This applies particularly when you are attempting to work out the answers to the number problems in the examples, and the practice tests given below. However, you can use a calculator at the end to check your answers – especially if you have run into difficulties.

Examples

The examples given below should help to give you an idea of what is involved before you start work on the practice tests. It is suggested that you work your way through the examples, writing your answers in the spaces provided. The answers are given in **Table 5.1.**

Example 1

How much would it cost to buy seven loaves of bread at 52p a loaf?

A	B	C	D	E
£3.44	£3.54	£3.64	£3.74	£3.84

Answer = ☐

Example 2

If I pay £4.56 for a tin of paint and 85p for a brush, how much will I have spent in total?

A	B	C	D	E
£5.31	£5.41	£5.51	£5.61	£5.71

Answer = ☐

Example 3

A car park holds 550 cars when it is full. How many cars does it hold when it is half full?

A	B	C	D	E
1100	250	55	275	350

Answer = ☐

Example 4

My bus journey to the station takes 35 minutes and my train journey then takes 55 minutes. How long does my journey take in total?

A	B	C	D	E
1½ hrs	1¼ hrs	70 min	45 min	85 min

Answer = ☐

Example 5

Out of 13,750 people in a football stadium, 10% are season ticket holders. How many people do not have a season ticket?

A	B	C	D	E
1,375	1,775	10,750	12,375	15,125

Answer = ☐

Example 6

Each pack of tiles contains enough tiles to cover 4 sq m. How many packs of tiles are needed to cover a floor that measures 40 m by 40 m?

A	B	C	D	E
440	20	200	40	400

Answer = ☐

Example 7

A survey samples 1 out of every 9 households. Out of 117 households, how many would be sampled?

A	B	C	D	E
10	11	12	13	14

Answer = ☐

Example 8

Four streets have the following number of houses in them: 18; 23; 41; 37. What is the average number of houses per street?

A	B	C	D	E
29.75	31.75	33	37.5	119

Answer = ☐

Example 9

A motorist is travelling at 72.5 mph in an area where the speed limit is 50 mph. By how much is the driver exceeding the speed limit?

A	B	C	D	E
20.5 mph	22.5 mph	52.5 mph	70.5 mph	120.5 mph

Answer = ☐

Example 10

How many 15-litre drums are needed to fill a 450-litre tank?

A	B	C	D	E
30	25	15	5	3

Answer = ☐

If you look closely at the number problems given in the above examples you will see that they are aimed at assessing your ability to use the four basic rules of arithmetic:

- addition;
- subtraction;
- multiplication;
- division.

In so doing, you are required to show that you are able to work in:

- whole numbers;
- fractions;
- decimals;
- averages;
- percentages;
- ratios (and proportions).

Finally, you have to be able to use the basic rules of arithmetic skills and different types of numbers in the calculation of:

- money;
- numbers of objects;
- speed;
- time;
- area;
- volume.

Table 5.1 shows how these principles have been applied in the examples given above, together with the answers.

Before moving on to the practice tests you should consider whether or not you need to revise your basic number skills. You can start this process by making use of the checklists given above. For each of the number skills in the lists, all you have to do is to decide how competent you think you are and record your decision in the appropriate box by writing a number, where:

1 = I am already good at this
2 = I can do this most of the time, but with some difficulty when under pressure
3 = I need to work on this to reach the required standard

Having done this, you should try to do some remedial work on any of the number skills that fall into category 2 or category 3. You can do this by working your way through the relevant

Table 5.1

Example	Answer	Basic rules of arithmetic	Types of numbers	Application
1	C	Multiplication	Decimals	Money
2	B	Addition	Decimals	Money
3	D	Multiplication or Division	Fractions	Objects (cars)
4	A	Addition	Whole numbers Fractions	Time
5	D	Division or Multiplication Subtraction	Whole numbers Percentages	Objects (people)
6	E	Multiplication Division	Whole numbers	Area
7	D	Division	Ratios	Objects (households)
8	A	Addition Division	Averages Decimals	Objects (houses)
9	B	Subtraction	Decimals	Speed
10	A	Division	Whole numbers	Liquids

sections of *How to Pass Numerical Reasoning Tests: A step-by-step guide to learning key numeracy skills* (revised edition) by Heidi Smith, published by Kogan Page. Building on your strengths (and in so doing addressing any weaknesses you might have) will have the advantage of improving your chances of doing well in the practice tests – and that should boost your confidence when the time comes to take the real test.

Once you feel ready to do so, move on to the numerical reasoning practice tests given below. Each test consists of **25 questions** for which you should allow yourself **12 minutes** per test. Work as quickly and as accurately as you can. Use a sheet of paper or a notepad for any rough work. If you are not sure of an answer, mark your best choice, but avoid wild guessing. If you want to change an answer, rub it out completely and then write your new answer in the space provided. The answers are given at the end of the chapter. Give yourself one mark for each correct answer, and make a note of the scores to see if you are improving from one test to another.

After each test, you should take some time to work your way through it item by item, making sure that you understand how to arrive at the correct answer. You should also check to see if there is a pattern to any errors you happen to be making – you might have a weakness, which will cost you marks unless you do something about it. If you want to do some extra preparation for the numerical reasoning test you will find additional examples in Chapter 4 (Number Problem Tests) of *How to Pass Numeracy Tests*, 4th edition (Tolley and Thomas, published by Kogan Page).

Test 1

1. How much will five tins of soup cost at 55p a tin?

A	B	C	D	E
£2.25	£2.55	£2.60	£2.75	£2.95

    Answer = ☐

2. A person saves £35 in four weeks. At this rate, how much will have been saved in one year?

A	B	C	D	E
£200	£250	£355	£420	£455

    Answer = ☐

3. What is the total cost of a journey when £1.65 is spent on bus-fares and an underground ticket costs £2.50?

A	B	C	D	E
£3.15	£3.60	£3.95	£4.05	£4.15

    Answer = ☐

4. What is the average number of people per car, when six cars carry 30 people?

A	B	C	D	E
4.5	5.0	5.5	6.0	6.5

    Answer = ☐

5. If shopping items cost £12.64, how much money remains out of £20?

A	B	C	D	E
£6.36	£6.63	£7.36	£7.46	£7.63

    Answer = ☐

6. A car is travelling at 64 mph. How many miles will it have travelled in 45 mins?

A	B	C	D	E
40	44	46	48	50

Answer = ☐

7. Six magazines contain 120 pages each. How many pages are there in total?

A	B	C	D	E
620	720	760	780	820

Answer = ☐

8. A researcher interviews one household out of every eight in a village of 240 households. How many interviews take place?

A	B	C	D	E
12	24	30	32	36

Answer = ☐

9. If my weekly paper bill is £3.20 and the delivery charge is an extra 35p, how much do I have to pay over six weeks?

A	B	C	D	E
£19.20	£19.65	£20.20	£20.30	£21.30

Answer = ☐

10. Items costing £2.50, £3.10, and £4.40 are bought out of the petty cash, which contains £30. What percentage of the cash is left?

A	B	C	D	E
30.33%	33.33%	60.50%	66.66%	77.77%

Answer = ☐

11. Number of foggy days

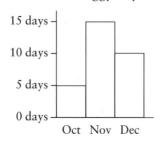

What is the average number of foggy days per month over this three-month period?

A	B	C	D	E
5	7.5	10	15	17.5

Answer = ☐

12. What is the average length of four pieces of wood, which measure 2.10 m, 1.80 m, 3.65 m and 2.45 m?

A	B	C	D	E
2.50 m	2.75 m	2.80 m	2.85 m	2.90 m

Answer = ☐

13. A customer withdraws £240 from her account. She gets half the money in £20 notes and the remainder in £10 notes. How many notes does she receive?

A	B	C	D	E
12	15	18	20	24

Answer = ☐

14. How many 568 ml cartons of milk are there in a chiller unit if the total quantity of milk being stored is 17.040 litres?

A	B	C	D	E
20	25	30	34	35

Answer = ☐

15. If 3 m of chain fencing are needed to link up two posts, what is the total length required to link up 10 posts?

A	B	C	D	E
20 m	27 m	30 m	32 m	36 m

Answer = ☐

16. A constable leaves the house at 08.00 hours and returns at 17.30 hours. How many hours has she been away from home?

A	B	C	D	E
8	8½	8¾	9½	10

Answer = ☐

17. A car park is full and contains 150 cars. If 40 cars are blue, 30 are white, 30 are green and the rest are red, then what percentage must be red?

A	B	C	D	E
25%	33.3%	50%	66.6%	70%

Answer = ☐

18. A street has 26 houses. Two houses receive five letters each, 10 receive three each and the rest get one each. How many letters have been delivered in total?

A	B	C	D	E
38	44	48	52	54

Answer = ☐

19. Five parcels of equal weight cost £16.25 to send by post. What is the cost per parcel?

A   B   C   D   E
£3.10   £3.15   £3.25   £3.75   £3.95

Answer = ☐

20. One carpet tile measures 50 cm by 50 cm. How many tiles are required to cover a floor that measures 5 m by 4 m?

A   B   C   D   E
80   85   90   94   100

Answer = ☐

21. If a person saves £40 a month out of a total wage of £1,000, then what percentage is being saved per month?

A   B   C   D   E
40%   10%   6%   15%   4%

Answer = ☐

22. If I walk to the local shops, which are 2,900 m from home, and call at the post office, which is ¾ of this distance, then how far away in metres is the post office from my home?

A   B   C   D   E
650   750   2,175   955   1,950

Answer = ☐

23. I hand over a £10 note at the supermarket checkout and receive £4.75 change, having bought three items of equal value. What was the price of a single item?

A	B	C	D	E
£1.33	£2.23	£2.17	£1.15	£1.75

Answer = ☐

24. How many hours will it take to drive to a destination 315 km from home and then return to my starting point, if I drive at 90 kph?

A	B	C	D	E
6	7	8	3	9

Answer = ☐

25. What is the average length in centimetres of four pieces of wood measuring 3.62 m, 2.42 m, 1.66 m and 4.90 m?

A	B	C	D	E
3.76	4.06	2.83	2.95	3.15

Answer = ☐

Test 2

1. If £15.43 is spent on leisure activities each week, then how much is spent in eight weeks?

A	B	C	D	E
£105.72	£110.72	£115.52	£121.24	£123.44

    Answer = ☐

2. If one copy of a report weighs 140 g, how many kilograms do 150 reports weigh?

A	B	C	D	E
19 kg	20 kg	21 kg	22 kg	23 kg

    Answer = ☐

3. A car journey of 325 miles takes 5 hours. What is the average speed of the car?

A	B	C	D	E
60 mph	65 mph	68 mph	70 mph	75 mph

    Answer = ☐

4. The total takings for a single theatrical performance amount to £4,720. If one seat costs £16, how many are in the audience?

A	B	C	D	E
255	260	275	295	300

    Answer = ☐

5. How many pieces of string, each measuring 1.5 m, can be cut from a ball that is 90 m long?

A	B	C	D	E
35	40	50	60	65

Answer = ☐

6. If 70% of £350 has been spent, how much money remains?

A	B	C	D	E
£105	£110	£115	£120	£125

Answer = ☐

7. An officer leaves home in his car at 07.30 hours and reaches his destination at 13.45 hours. How long is it since he left his house?

A	B	C	D	E
6 hrs	6¼ hrs	6½ hrs	7 hrs	7¼ hrs

Answer = ☐

8. If one ticket costs £4.20, how much will it cost for a party of nine?

A	B	C	D	E
£37.50	£37.80	£38.50	£39	£39.80

Answer = ☐

9. 25% of 180 people attending a function are smokers. How many are non-smokers?

A	B	C	D	E
45	75	90	130	135

Answer = ☐

10. The combined weekly wages for a family contain four £100 notes, three £50 notes, six £20 notes and five £1 coins. How much does the family earn in a week?

A	B	C	D	E
£575	£595	£655	£675	£685

Answer = ☐

11. If I begin an eight-hour shift at 08.30 and do one hour overtime, what time will I finish work?

A	B	C	D	E
16.30	17.00	17.30	18.00	18.30

Answer = ☐

12. A room measures 6 m by 4.5 m and has two doorways each 90 cm wide. What length of skirting board is required?

A	B	C	D	E
18.20 m	19.20 m	19.80 m	20.20 m	21.00 m

Answer = ☐

13. If eight notepads cost £6.08, how much is the price of one pad?

A	B	C	D	E
76p	78p	80p	81p	82p

Answer = ☐

14. A printing machine produces 30 pages per minute. At this rate, how long will it take to print a 360-page document?

A	B	C	D	E
10 min	12 min	13 min	15 min	16 min

Answer = ☐

15. A set meal in a restaurant costs £5.60. If senior citizens are given a 5% reduction, what will the bill amount to if 10 senior citizens have such a meal?

A	B	C	D	E
£55.30	£54.20	£53.60	£53.20	£52.90

Answer = ☐

16. If braid costs 56p a metre, how much will 20 m of braid cost?

A	B	C	D	E
£12.12	£11.56	£11.20	£10.80	£10.56

Answer = ☐

17. Items totalling £260 were purchased by writing a cheque for £46 and adding £63 to a store account. How much cash was used to pay for the remaining amount?

A	B	C	D	E
£171	£165	£161	£155	£151

Answer = ☐

18. If I jog every day for 30 minutes, how much time do I spend jogging in seven days?

A	B	C	D	E
2½ hr	2¾ hr	3 hr	3½ hr	3¾ hr

Answer = ☐

19. The garden shown below has two vegetable plots and a path 2 m wide. What area of turf would be required to cover the plots?

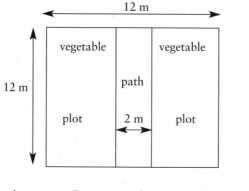

A   B   C   D   E
50 m²   100 m²   120 m²   125 m²   140 m²

Answer = ☐

20. The petrol tank of a car has a maximum capacity of 48 l. If the tank is a quarter full, how many litres of petrol are needed to fill it to maximum?

A   B   C   D   E
12   26   28   34   36

Answer = ☐

21. What percentage of £50 is £15?

A   B   C   D   E
10%   30%   15%   20%   25%

Answer = ☐

22. How many square metres of carpet are needed to cover one floor measuring 6.5 m × 7.0 m and another measuring 3.5 m × 5.0 m?

A	B	C	D	E
63	58.5	56	66	50

Answer = ☐

23. If I make a journey which is 480 km long, and it takes five hours, then what is my average speed in kilometres per hour?

A	B	C	D	E
90	86	96	84	94

Answer = ☐

24. If a chicken weighs 1.75 kg and the recommended cooking time is 20 minutes per 0.5 kg plus 20 minutes, then how long will the chicken have to be in the oven in minutes?

A	B	C	D	E
60	75	80	90	65

Answer = ☐

25. If a bus is carrying 36 passengers, a ferry 205 people and an aeroplane 194 tourists, then what is the average number of people carried by these three methods of transport?

A	B	C	D	E
154	145	435	165	180

Answer = ☐

Test 3

1. If three accidents occur on average every two days at a crossroads, how many accidents will occur on average every eight days?

A	B	C	D	E
4	6	8	12	16

    Answer = ☐

2. One case containing 12 bottles of wine costs £48. How much will three bottles cost?

A	B	C	D	E
£11	£12	£14	£16	£18

    Answer = ☐

3. A health club raises its annual subscription of £240 by 15%. What will the new subscription cost?

A	B	C	D	E
£255	£260	£266	£276	£312

    Answer = ☐

4. If I spend £1.50, £2.05 and £3.20 on items for lunch, how much have I spent in total?

A	B	C	D	E
£6.55	£6.65	£6.75	£6.85	£7.05

    Answer = ☐

5. An investor withdraws 40% of her savings from an account, which holds £800. How much remains in the account?

A	B	C	D	E
£480	£460	£420	£320	£310

Answer = ☐

6. A stolen wallet contains two £100 notes, seven £50 notes, three £10 notes, two £5 notes and 75p in coins. How much money has been stolen?

A	B	C	D	E
£555.75	£560.75	£570.75	£580.75	£590.75

Answer = ☐

7. If 20 pages of a 240-page notepad are used every day, how many days will it be until a replacement pad is needed?

A	B	C	D	E
6	10	11	12	13

Answer = ☐

8. How much does it cost to buy 14 box files at £3.50 each?

A	B	C	D	E
£48.50	£49	£49.50	£50	£53.50

Answer = ☐

9. What sum of money remains if I started with £25 in my wallet and I spent £13.36?

A	B	C	D	E
£10.64	£10.74	£11.64	£12.46	£12.64

Answer = ☐

10. If I go on duty at 14.30 and finish at 22.30, how many hours will I have worked in five days?

A   B   C   D   E
30 hr   35 hr   40 hr   42 hr   44 hr

Answer = ☐

11. What is the total paved area of the garden shown below?

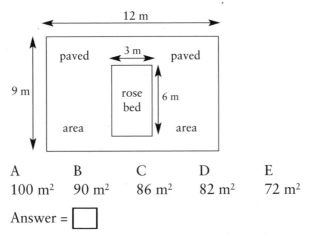

A   B   C   D   E
100 m²   90 m²   86 m²   82 m²   72 m²

Answer = ☐

12. What is the total weight of five packages each of 100 g and six parcels each of 7.5 kg?

A   B   C   D   E
36.5 kg   40.5 kg   42.5 kg   45.5 kg   50.5 kg

Answer = ☐

13. If seven people gave taped interviews, which lasted 1 hr 24 mins in total, what was the length of one interview on average?

A   B   C   D   E
12 min   13 min   14 min   15 min   16 min

Answer = ☐

14. If the number of season ticket holders has fallen by ¹/₈ to 10,500, how many season ticket holders have been lost?

A	B	C	D	E
1,300	1,400	1,500	1,650	1,700

Answer = ☐

15. What is the average height of a group of people if two are 1.77 m tall, three are 1.92 m tall and one is 2.10 m tall?

A	B	C	D	E
1.79 m	1.81 m	1.84 m	1.87 m	1.90 m

Answer = ☐

16. If a motorist is travelling at 56 mph in a built-up area, where the speed limit is 30 mph, by how much should the speed of the car be reduced?

A	B	C	D	E
17 mph	24 mph	26 mph	27 mph	28 mph

Answer = ☐

17. A box of decorations which cost £30 last Christmas is reduced in price by 12%. What is the revised price?

A	B	C	D	E
£25.40	£25.60	£26.40	£26.80	£26.90

Answer = ☐

18. A person who works a five-day week has been absent for 21 full days and eight half-days. How many weeks of work have been missed in total?

A	B	C	D	E
4	5	5.5	6	6.5

Answer = ☐

19. One vehicle in 15 is stopped in a traffic survey. How many vehicles will have been stopped out of 225?

A	B	C	D	E
11	12	13	14	15

Answer = ☐

20. If a drum can hold 120 l of paraffin, how much will it cost to fill the empty drum when paraffin is priced at £1.99 for 4 l?

A	B	C	D	E
£58.30	£58.60	£59.70	£59.90	£60.30

Answer = ☐

21. How many pieces of ribbon each 50 cm long can be cut from a roll that is 10 m in length?

A	B	C	D	E
5	50	20	15	25

Answer = ☐

22. A theatre with the capacity to hold an audience of 500 people has an attendance of 450 on an opening night. As a percentage of the capacity audience, how many more people could have attended?

A	B	C	D	E
10%	15%	46%	8%	14%

Answer = ☐

23. A cleaner works at office A for five hours a day and office B for two hours daily for five days a week. How many hours will the cleaner have worked in four weeks?

A	B	C	D	E
70	140	90	150	105

Answer = ☐

24. A store has a sale that reduces all goods by 10%. How much will I save in total on items that cost £6.60, £23.45 and £10.75?

A	B	C	D	E
£4.80	£5.80	£5.08	£4.08	£3.90

Answer = ☐

25. If one in 12 people are wearing blue rosettes, how many blue rosettes will there be in a crowd of 1,728 people?

A	B	C	D	E
114	182	144	172	126

Answer = ☐

Test 4

1. A pack of four tins of beans is usually priced at £1.44. If a special deal offers one of the tins free, then how much would the pack cost now?

A	B	C	D	E
£1.18	£1.10	£1.08	99p	£1.02

    Answer = ☐

2. If a person has watched television for 1 hr 35 min in the morning and then for 2 hr 25 min during the rest of the day, what fraction of time has been spent watching television over a 24-hour period?

A	B	C	D	E
$1/3$	$1/8$	$1/4$	$1/6$	$1/5$

    Answer = ☐

3. How much is the cost of buying three boxes of teabags at £1.69 each?

A	B	C	D	E
£5.10	£4.17	£5.07	£4.98	£4.97

    Answer = ☐

4. If two-thirds of the eggs on a chicken farm have already hatched and the flock is expected to total 1,800, then how many eggs are there still to hatch?

A	B	C	D	E
1,200	800	900	1,100	600

    Answer = ☐

5. Theatre tickets cost £15 for an adult, with senior citizens being allowed a £1 reduction. A child's ticket costs half that of an adult. What is the total bill if two adults, two children and two senior citizens visit the theatre?

A	B	C	D	E
£63	£73	£59	£72	£69

Answer = ☐

6. One in every eight tins of soup is sold from a shelf originally displaying 120. How many tins will be needed to restock the shelf?

A	B	C	D	E
12	15	14	20	8

Answer = ☐

7. A cyclist returns home at 16.30 hours after a six-hour ride and a one-hour break. What time did the cyclist set out?

A	B	C	D	E
10.30	11.30	11.00	10.00	09.30

Answer = ☐

8. How long have I spent exercising, in minutes, if I lift weights for 10 min, cycle for 1 hr and then swim for 15 min?

A	B	C	D	E
45	40	85	75	60

Answer = ☐

9. If I buy some apples for 99p, sparkling water for 58p and a bottle of wine costing £5.44, how much have I spent in total?

A	B	C	D	E
£7.01	£6.01	£6.94	£7.10	£7.32

Answer = ☐

10. A bus journey takes 1 hr 30 min, followed by a journey of half that time. What is the total length of travelling time in minutes?

A	B	C	D	E
125	120	135	140	130

Answer = ☐

11. A motorist is travelling at 68 mph and then reduces the speed by a quarter. What is the speed in mph now?

A	B	C	D	E
17	51	18	56	48

Answer = ☐

12. A road has 180 houses, 40% of which have a white gate. How many houses have gates painted in a colour other than white?

A	B	C	D	E
72	74	108	104	36

Answer = ☐

13. If a teenager makes £38 a week doing a paper-round and in addition is given £12 in pocket money, how much will he make in six weeks?

A   B   C   D   E
£360   £288   £320   £300   £290

Answer = ☐

14. A school of 760 pupils is hit by an influenza epidemic reducing full attendance to half. How many pupils will be present?

A   B   C   D   E
330   325   280   375   380

Answer = ☐

15. If I cycle 69 km in 3 hours, what is my average speed?

A   B   C   D   E
32 kph   23 kph   35 kph   29 kph   34 kph

Answer = ☐

16. If a tourist information centre is asked about holiday accommodation on average eight times a day, how many such enquiries will be answered on average in 14 days?

A   B   C   D   E
56   84   22   108   112

Answer = ☐

17. A box containing six bottles of wine costs £39. How much will four bottles cost?

A   B   C   D   E
£23   £28.50   £17.50   £26   £18.50

Answer = ☐

18. If I withdraw £25 from a cash point and spend £17.25, how much have I left?

A	B	C	D	E
£2.75	£7.75	£6.75	£7.25	£6.25

Answer = [　]

19. A pane of glass measures 0.5 × 0.5 m. How many panes are needed to glaze a window area 5 m × 5 m?

A	B	C	D	E
250	175	100	50	125

Answer = [　]

20. A roll of turf is 60 cm wide. How many widths of turf are needed to cover a garden that is 6 m wide?

A	B	C	D	E
6	60	100	50	10

Answer = [　]

21. If a young girl practises her violin for one hour a day and plays football for two hours every week, then how many hours does she spend on these activities over 28 days?

A	B	C	D	E
32	36	38	40	42

Answer = [　]

22. If a bottle of oil holds 1.5 l, then how many litres in total do 25 bottles hold?

A	B	C	D	E
37.5	35.5	27.0	26.5	25.5

Answer = [　]

23. A jacket originally costing £150 is reduced in a sale by 20%. How much is the sale price?

A £100   B £95   C £125   D £130   E £120

Answer = ☐

24. If I start work at 08.30 and finish at 16.30 with one hour for lunch, how many hours will I have worked over three five-day weeks?

A 90   B 80   C 105   D 95   E 85

Answer = ☐

25. If a sweater costs £35.50, what would three sweaters cost?

A £105   B £71   C £95   D £106.50   E £100.50

Answer = ☐

Test 5

1. The cost of your car insurance increases by 15%. If the annual cost was £280 before the increase, how much is the new cost?

A £320   B £42   C £322   D £295   E £342

Answer = ☐

2. If you exercise for 45 min each day, how much time do you spend exercising in nine days?

A	B	C	D	E
6:35 hrs	7:15 hrs	6:55 hrs	6:25 hrs	6:15 hrs

Answer = ☐

3. Senior citizens are given a discount of 20% on tickets for a concert, which cost £30 each. How much change in total would a group of four receive if they tendered £100?

A	B	C	D	E
£35	£3.50	£40	£4.00	£4.40

Answer = ☐

4. If a motorcycle travels at an average speed of 54 mph, how many miles will it have travelled after 40 min?

A	B	C	D	E
36	32	42	46	38

Answer = ☐

5. What is the average score per dart of a darts player who throws six darts and scores the following: 109, 84, 47, 123, 114, and 15?

A	B	C	D	E
72	75	80	82	86

Answer = ☐

6. An e-mail had been sent at 7:19; the clock on the computer said it was now 13.24. How long has it been since the e-mail was sent?

A	B	C	D	E
6:05 hr	6:15 hr	6:25 hr	6:35 hr	6:45 hr

Answer = ☐

7. You start to read a book at 22.20 and by 23.00 you have read 30 pages. If you continued reading until 23.20 at the same speed how many additional pages would you have read?

A	B	C	D	E
1.5	10	12	15	20

Answer = ☐

8. The table given below shows the time of sunrise and sunset for five cities (V-Z) in the UK for a day in mid-May. Which of the five cities has the shortest period of daylight?

City	Sunrise	Sunset
V	5.08	20.58
W	5.16	20.57
X	5.22	21.21
Y	5.02	21.03
Z	5.06	20.56

A	B	C	D	E
V	W	X	Y	Z

Answer = ☐

9. A supermarket car park has spaces for 680 cars. How many empty spaces will there be when five out of every eight spaces are occupied?

A	B	C	D	E
255	275	325	375	425

Answer = ☐

10. If it takes 1l of emulsion paint to cover an area of wall measuring 6 m by 3 m, how many litres of paint will be needed to cover an area of wall which measures 9 m by 7 m?

A	B	C	D	E
5.5	5	4.5	4	3.5

Answer = ☐

11. Ninety-four vehicles were halted as part of a traffic survey in order to question the drivers. How many vehicles in total passed the checkpoint if every sixth vehicle was stopped?

A	B	C	D	E
944	764	564	464	364

Answer = ☐

12. Two hundred and twenty chairs were put out in a hall for a public meeting. If 176 people attended the meeting, what percentage of the chairs would not have been used?

A	B	C	D	E
18%	20%	22%	24%	26%

Answer = ☐

13. If your telephone bills for the first three quarters of the year are £74.45, £69.72 and £83.53, how much have you spent per month on average?

A	B	C	D	E
£23.50	£24.30	£27.40	£25.30	£26.75

Answer = ☐

14. A hosepipe discharges water at a rate of 5 gallons per minute. How long, in minutes, will it take to fill a garden pond with a capacity of 230 gallons from empty?

A	B	C	D	E
46	48	50	44	42

Answer = ☐

15. The perimeter of a local park measures 6.5 kms and it takes a runner 3 hrs to run round it four times. What is the runner's average speed in kilometres per hour?

A	B	C	D	E
7.33	7.86	8.33	8.66	9.33

Answer = ☐

16. The number of people questioned by a team of six police officers as part of a house-to-house investigation was as follows: 35; 23; 44; 19; 26; 21. What is the average number of people questioned per team member?

A	B	C	D	E
25	26.5	27	27.7	28

Answer = ☐

17. In an atlas, ½ cm represents a distance of 250 miles on a map of the world. What is the distance represented by 2¼ cm on the same map?

A	B	C	D	E
1025	1075	1125	1200	1275

Answer = ☐

18. Two groups of friends have shares in a winning lottery ticket. In Group A there are five members and in Group B there are four; irrespective of which group they are in, each individual gets an equal share of the winnings. If Group A receives a total of £450, how much does Group B receive?

A	B	C	D	E
£400	£425	£395	£360	£345

Answer = ☐

19. If a car dealer buys a second-hand car for £4,800 and then sells it for £5,400, what is the percentage profit on the transaction?

A	B	C	D	E
12.5%	13%	13.5%	14%	14.5%

Answer = ☐

20. Two people walk along a coastal footpath at a rate of 4.5 mph. After walking for 2½ hrs they still have eight miles left to complete their walk. What is the total distance they plan to walk?

A	B	C	D	E
20.50	22.25	18.75	19.25	19.75

Answer = ☐

21. If a traffic warden discovered that eight out of 178 cars in a car park were not displaying a valid parking ticket, what percentage of the total is that?

A	B	C	D	E
2.8%	3.6%	4.5%	5.2%	5.7%

Answer = ☐

22. The fuel tank of a car can hold a maximum of 65 l. If it already contains 7 l, how much would it cost the driver to fill it up with fuel costing 98p per litre?

A   B   C   D   E
£58.64   £56.84   £55.80   £53.92   £57.46

Answer = ☐

23. Three separate calls on a mobile phone last 9 min, 7 min, and 4 min. If the first minute of each call costs 25p and all of the other time is charged at 5p per minute, how much in total did the three calls cost?

A   B   C   D   E
£1.60   £2.40   £1.85   £1.40   £2.20

Answer = ☐

24. A delivery van is carrying five boxes weighing 103 kg in total plus nine parcels weighing 14 kg each. What is the total weight of the load the delivery van is carrying?

A   B   C   D   E
619 kg   603 kg   629 kg   640 kg   641 kg

Answer = ☐

25. One carpet tile measures 50 cm by 50 cm and they can only be purchased in boxes containing 10 tiles each. How many boxes of carpet tiles would be needed to cover the floor of a room measuring 6 m by 5 m?

A   B   C   D   E
120   14   300   12   24

Answer = ☐

Answers to numerical reasoning tests

Test 1 (page 46)		Test 2 (page 52)		Test 3 (page 58)		Test 4 (page 64)		Test 5 (page 69)	
1	D	1	E	1	D	1	C	1	C
2	D	2	C	2	B	2	D	2	B
3	E	3	B	3	D	3	C	3	D
4	B	4	D	4	C	4	E	4	A
5	C	5	D	5	A	5	B	5	D
6	D	6	A	6	E	6	B	6	A
7	B	7	B	7	D	7	E	7	D
8	C	8	B	8	B	8	C	8	B
9	E	9	E	9	C	9	A	9	E
10	D	10	D	10	C	10	C	10	E
11	C	11	C	11	B	11	B	11	C
12	A	12	B	12	D	12	C	12	B
13	C	13	A	13	A	13	D	13	D
14	C	14	B	14	C	14	E	14	A
15	B	15	D	15	E	15	B	15	D
16	D	16	C	16	C	16	E	16	E
17	B	17	E	17	C	17	D	17	C
18	E	18	D	18	B	18	B	18	D
19	C	19	C	19	E	19	C	19	A
20	A	20	E	20	C	20	E	20	D
21	E	21	B	21	C	21	B	21	C
22	C	22	A	22	A	22	A	22	B
23	E	23	C	23	B	23	E	23	A
24	B	24	D	24	D	24	C	24	E
25	E	25	B	25	C	25	D	25	D

6

Verbal logical reasoning test

Introduction

In this test you are given a set of descriptions of imaginary events (or 'scenarios'), which resemble those encountered by police officers in the course of their duties, together with additional facts which are known about them. In each case they are followed by a number of conclusions, which might be derived from the information provided. Your task is to evaluate each of the conclusions given, and then, in the light of the evidence, decide if:

A   The conclusion is **true** given the situation described and the facts which are known about it.

B   The conclusion is **false** given the situation described and the facts which are known about it.

C   It is **impossible to say** whether the conclusion is true or false given the situation described and the facts which are known about it.

In order to get a better idea of what you have to do, take a look at the example given below:

■ Read the information provided.
■ Evaluate each of the five conclusions.
■ Using a pencil, mark your answer A, B or C in the answer boxes provided.
■ Check your answers against those given below.

Example

Brian Jones aged 10 and Ben Wilson aged 12 were reported missing at 20.00 on 9 May after they failed to return home from a cycle ride to some nearby woods. The police have set up a search party for the two missing boys. It is also known that:

■ The woods are very dense and over 10 ha in area.
■ The two boys were admitted to a local hospital at 17.00.
■ Brian Jones lived with his stepmother.
■ Ben Wilson was an only child living with his father.
■ Ben had a new 10-gear racing bike.
■ The wood has several ponds and swampy areas.
■ The older students picked on Brian at school.
■ Ben saw an educational psychologist at school each week.

1. The two boys could have run away from home.   ☐
2. The two boys had a cycle accident and were taken to hospital.   ☐
3. The older students had picked on Brian in the woods.   ☐
4. Ben had no brothers or sisters.   ☐
5. Ben had no problems at school or at home.   ☐

Answers

1 = A   2 = C   3 = C   4 = A   5 = B

In the verbal logical reasoning test you will be given six scenarios like the one given in the example. Each one will be accompanied by a list of known facts followed by a set of conclusions for you to evaluate. Although the information provided will be different in each case, when you look closely at them you will see that they have many things in common. For example, they will all provide you with evidence related to:

- **WHAT** happened, ie descriptions of the imaginary events.
- **WHO** was involved, ie information concerning the people involved.
- **WHEN** the events took place, ie dates and times.
- **WHERE** the events occurred, ie places and locations.

The ability to see the connections between these different categories of information – and not to view them in isolation from each other – is vital in this type of test. For example, in order to reach the right conclusion you may have to work out if a named person could have been in the place where something happened at the time when it is known to have occurred. The 'clues', which will enable you to get the right answer, will all be there in the text – all you have to do is to find them and interpret them correctly. However, you will also find that some of the information provided is relevant to the conclusions you are being asked to reach, and that some of it is irrelevant. In fact some things may have been deliberately inserted to divert your attention in the wrong direction – a so-called 'distracter'.

You will also have to cope with information which has been presented in such a way as to lead you into making false assumptions. For example, you might be told that a person is known to have been inside the local pub all evening and that they were seen to stagger and fall down on leaving. It would be easy to conclude that the person had been drinking all evening and had fallen down because they were drunk. However, 'given the situation described and the facts which are known about it' there is a perfectly logical alternative explanation. For example, the person could have been drinking non-alcoholic drinks all evening, and tripped and fallen as a result of a loose paving stone.

In order to do well in verbal logical reasoning tests, therefore, you have to be able to study the information provided with these things in mind – and under severe time pressure. So, here is a summary of what you should try to do:

- Read the information quickly, noting the what, who, when and where, in order to get an overall sense of what the scenario is about.
- Try to detect the information which is relevant from that which has been put there to distract you.
- In relation to each item, scan the text for the information you need to answer the question correctly.

Five practice tests of this type are given below. Each test contains **31 questions** and you should allow yourself **25 minutes** per test. Work as quickly and accurately as you can. If you are not sure of an answer, mark your best choice, but avoid wild guessing. If you want to change an answer, rub it out completely and then write your new answer in the appropriate box. Give yourself one mark for each correct answer and make a note of your scores to see if you are improving from one test to another.

It should be pointed out that all of the names and situations used in the examples of verbal logical reasoning tests in this chapter are fictitious. Consequently, any resemblance they may bear to real persons, places or events is coincidental.

Finally, if you want some extra preparation for the verbal logical reasoning test you will find additional examples in Chapter 10 of *How to Pass Verbal Reasoning Tests*, 4th edition (Tolley and Thomas), which is published by Kogan Page.

Test 1

> At 19.05 on 12 December there was a loud explosion in 2 Bathurst Street. A woman and child managed to escape from the house unhurt, but the ensuing fire claimed the lives of an elderly man and young baby. It is also known that:
>
> - John Watts, aged 91, owned 2 Bathurst Street.
> - A smell of gas had been reported at 15.00 on 12 December from 2 Bathurst Street.
> - The police informed Fred Watts at 20.30 on 12 December of the death at 2 Bathurst Street of his baby son George Watts and his father John Watts.
> - Fred Watts works nightshift at a local factory.
> - Fred Watts is a divorcee.

1. The explosion at 2 Bathurst Street on 12 December was due to a leaking gas pipe. □

2. Fred Watts was married to the woman who escaped safely from the explosion. □

3. The police took less than two hours to find the house-owner's son. □

4. A gas leak could have been the reason for the explosion. □

5. John Watts was not a grandfather. □

At 02.20 on Tuesday, a four-wheel-drive vehicle plunged over the edge of a steep mountain pass and burst into flames as it reached the valley bottom. There were no survivors. The sole victim has been identified as Mr John Joseph Broon of Muckty, a village 3 km from the scene of the accident. It is also known that:

- John Broon was an alcoholic who had sought help from Alcoholics Anonymous.
- John Broon had been at the local pub from 18.00 on Monday to 02.10 on Tuesday.
- John Broon had a wife and two children.
- The barperson at the local pub had served John all night.
- The drive from the local pub to John's house took 15 minutes along a narrow twisty road, which hugged the mountainside.
- A dead sheep was found on the side of the valley, 100 metres from where the car left the road.

6. John Broon was on his way home when he was killed. ☐

7. John Broon had swerved to miss a sheep on the narrow road and had gone over the edge of the valley side. ☐

8. John Broon was the only person in the car when it crashed. ☐

9. The alcohol content of John Broon at 02.20 would have been over the legal limit. ☐

10. John Broon had eaten a large supper at home with his wife and two children at 21.00 on Monday. ☐

The new sports club at Dolchem was vandalized on Friday evening after the boy scouts had finished their weekly meeting in the new hall. Damages are expected to be over £4,000. It is also known that:

- The Parish Council was in debt after the construction of the new sports club.
- Local teenagers opposed the proposal to charge people to use the club's facilities.
- The boy scouts have abandoned the old village hall where they used to have their meetings.
- There is a high level of youth unemployment in Dolchem.
- Witnesses saw a group of five youths running away from the club at 21.30 on Friday.
- Spray cans were used on the club walls, liquid paint and faeces were deposited on the floor and windows were smashed.

11. Five young men were seen running away from the club at 21.30 on Friday. ☐

12. The boy scouts are willing to pay to use the new club. ☐

13. The youth of Dolchem had a motive to vandalize the new sports club. ☐

14. The Parish Council had profited from the construction of the new sports club. ☐

15. The idea of charging people to use the new sports facilities had caused some opposition amongst the younger members of the community. ☐

A night watchman was attacked when a fuel depot in Netherwich was broken into on 24 December and cash was stolen. A police spokesman said that Bill Sykes, a local man, had been taken into custody on 26 December, and was 'assisting them with their enquiries' into what could only be described as a 'violent but amateurish crime'. It is also known that:

- Bill Sykes has been living with his girlfriend Nancy.
- Bill Sykes is the owner of a bull terrier dog.
- The night watchman was distracted by the barking of a dog, and was hit over the head from behind.
- Sykes is already under a community service order for demanding money with menaces from his estranged wife.
- Since 31 December Mrs Sykes has complained that her husband had been pestering her to provide him with an alibi for 24 December.

16. Bill Sykes broke into the fuel depot and hit the night watchman over the head. ☐

17. Sykes stole the money from the fuel depot to give to his wife. ☐

18. Sykes has already been given an opportunity to avoid a custodial sentence. ☐

19. Sykes's girlfriend Nancy hit the night watchman over the head. ☐

20. The burglary was well planned and professionally executed. ☐

At 16.05 on Sunday 3 June, an elderly man was found dead in Cuthbert Park. His right-hand wrist had been slashed. The park keeper had seen a young man running out of the park at 15.30. The following facts are known:

- The park had been shut for major landscape changes.
- The young man was employed by the landscape contractors and worked in the park.
- The dead man had been diagnosed with terminal cancer on Friday 1 June.
- The landscape contractors do not work on Sundays.
- The park keeper is profoundly deaf.
- A sharp knife with a 16-centimetre blade was found 100 metres from the dead body.
- The victim was right-handed.

21. The park keeper heard a scream from inside the park at 15.25 on Sunday 3 June. ☐

22. The victim may have committed suicide. ☐

23. The young man seen running out of the park had just clocked off from his work with the landscape contractors. ☐

24. The knife found 100 metres from the body had been used to slash the victim's wrist. ☐

25. The victim had been mugged and stabbed by the young man. ☐

Following their success in the neighbouring towns of Barnford and Littleton, surveillance cameras are to be installed in the centre of Darton. Both the police and the City Council are convinced that public order offences can be reduced by the adoption of such a scheme. Although the Chamber of Commerce has voiced its support, representatives of civil liberties groups have expressed their concerns, claiming that it will be another case of 'Big Brother is watching you'. The following facts are also known:

- The cameras will be monitored on a random basis.
- The total number of thefts in the area to be covered by the scheme in the centre of Darton in 2008 was 1,905 and the total number of crimes was recorded at 3,646.
- It is estimated that the surveillance system will cost £100,000 to install and that staffing costs will be £80,000 per year.
- The City Council and the police have had many letters of support from local residents and representatives of local businesses.

26. Surveillance cameras have been a success in Darton. ☐

27. There is evidence that crime will be reduced in the centre of Darton by the use of surveillance cameras. ☐

28. For reasons of crime prevention, the police will constantly monitor the new surveillance system. ☐

29. In 2008 over half of the recorded crimes in the centre of Darton were thefts. ☐

30. There is unanimous support for the use of surveillance cameras in the centre of Darton. ☐

31. The new surveillance system will cost around £180,000 for the first year. ☐

Test 2

Joan Verse left her one-year-old daughter in the pram outside the butcher's as she went into the shop at 11.15 on Thursday 4 February. When she emerged neither the pram nor the baby were there. She rang the police on her mobile phone and reported the theft of her daughter at 11.30. A reliable witness saw a very tall, thin young man running down the street carrying a young baby that same morning at 11.20. It is also known that:

- The butcher's shop is on a steep hill.
- Joan Verse is divorced with two children.
- It was extremely icy underfoot and temperatures were below freezing.
- Joan Verse was in the process of fighting for custody of her child with her ex-husband.
- Joan was tall and her ex-husband was shorter than her and overweight.
- The pram was over 11 years old.
- Joan was having an affair with the college-student son of one of her neighbours.
- Downhill, the street led to the village pond, 40 metres from the newsagent's shop.

1. The baby girl had been kidnapped. ☐
2. The college student may be the father of the missing one-year-old girl. ☐
3. Joan's ex-husband was seen running down the street carrying a young baby on 4 February. ☐
4. The brakes on the pram could have failed, causing the pram to slide out of control down the street and across the frozen pond. ☐
5. Joan Verse was a vegetarian. ☐

On Saturday 12 May at 09.30 the groundsman at Dithcote Cricket Club discovered that the wickets had been vandalized and that the turf had been dug up and removed. The afternoon match between teams drawn from the members of the Conservative Club and the Round Table had to be cancelled. By Sunday it was evident that weedkiller had been used on the pitch and had been spread in the shape of the CND symbol. It is also known that:

- The groundsman is in sole charge of entry into the grounds of Dithcote Cricket Club.
- The Conservative Party had a majority on Dithcote Council.
- The local Conservative MP broke his leg on Thursday 10 May.
- The groundsman is a supporter of Greenpeace.
- A campaign to make Dithcote a nuclear-free zone had recently ended in failure.
- Brian Agler is the local Conservative MP.
- Brian Agler had played first-class cricket for his county.

6. The Conservative Party had blocked the recent campaign to make Dithcote a nuclear-free zone. ☐

7. The vandals may have broken into the cricket ground. ☐

8. Had the game gone ahead on Saturday 12 May, Brian Agler would have opened the batting for the Conservative Club eleven. ☐

9. The groundsman may have known the people who vandalized the cricket ground. ☐

10. Brian Agler is a known supporter of the policies of right-wing extremist groups. ☐

A 19-year-old male was found unconscious in his flat on 28 December at 23.00. He was taken immediately to hospital where his stomach was pumped. Although he regained consciousness he died shortly afterwards. Neighbours recall seeing various young people going into the flat at all hours of the day and night. Other facts known at this stage are:

- Peter Graick was a heroin addict.
- Empty bottles of spirits and paracetamol were found in the flat.
- Jo Hager supplied Peter with hard drugs.
- Peter used to frequent the local nightclub.
- Jo was the father of a two-month-old child.
- Jo's child was in care and had been tested HIV positive.
- The victim was a compulsive gambler.
- The victim had bruises on his head.

11. The victim was homeless. ☐

12. Peter died of an overdose of drugs. ☐

13. Neighbours may have seen Jo Hager enter the flat where the victim was found. ☐

14. The victim's child was in care. ☐

15. The neighbours took the victim to hospital. ☐

A mountain bike, which cost Peter Clarke £300, was stolen from outside the 'Freewheel' cycle shop in Langton High Street at 11.00 on 18 June. Peter, an unemployed factory worker, bought the bike to deliver the charity newspaper 'Good Neighbour News'. Reports on local radio of an increase in the number of recorded thefts of mountain bikes in Langton had prompted him to visit the cycle shop to buy a security lock. It is also known that:

- The police are questioning two youths who have been offering a mountain bike for sale in local pubs.
- A similar bike was later found partially submerged in the lake in Central Park.
- Mr Clarke has offered a reward of £30 for information leading to the recovery of his bicycle.
- Mr Clarke has decided to hire a bike from the 'Freewheel' cycle shop to help him with his newspaper deliveries.

16. Peter Clarke paid £300 for a mountain bike. ☐

17. Peter Clarke's stolen mountain bike was later found dumped in the lake in Central Park. ☐

18. Peter Clarke had saved up for the bike from his weekly earnings. ☐

19. A local landlord had assisted the police with their enquiries. ☐

20. Peter Clarke's mountain bike had been offered for sale by the two youths who are being questioned by the police. ☐

Between 12 March and 3 April there have been a number of cases of food poisoning at the old people's care home. It has resulted in two deaths, permanent paralysis of one old woman and continued hospitalization of three other residents. The police are treating the cases as suspicious. It is also known that:

▨ The residents have all agreed to leave 5% of their estates to the home on their death.

▨ The home is privately owned and run by David John.

▨ There have been delays of at least 28 hours from the appearance of the initial symptoms in reporting the cases of food poisoning.

▨ David John is a member of Alcoholics Anonymous.

▨ Janet Scree is the nurse in charge of the residents.

▨ David John is a qualified pharmacist.

▨ The care home is currently running at a loss.

▨ The chef ensures that the standards of hygiene in the kitchen are above the level required by environmental health inspectors.

▨ Janet Scree is colour-blind.

21. The residents of the care home suffering from food poisoning were treated in the same hospital. ☐

22. Janet Scree may have muddled up the residents' medicines. ☐

23. The care home will profit from the two deaths which have occurred. ☐

24. The kitchen staff worked in hygienic conditions. ☐

25. The victims were taken to hospital as soon as their symptoms appeared. ☐

Ron Study, a 20-year-old university student, was involved in a road accident on Friday night on the A1 in North Yorkshire. According to police, the accident occurred on the southbound carriageway at about 23.20. They said that the patrol car had been sent to the scene following a phone call they had received at 23.10 from a motorist who said that she had just seen two people walking along the side of the A1 South. It is also known that:

- Ron Study and Martin Less had been to a party at which they had been seen to be drinking heavily.
- They were almost knocked down as they attempted to cross the carriageway to get to the Easy Eater service area.
- Ron Study said that he had fallen asleep in a lay-by until he sobered up.
- He also said that he was awakened by blue flashing lights and realized that there must have been an accident.
- The driver of a car, which had been overtaking a lorry, said that he heard a thud and the lorry swerved towards him. He had managed to avoid a collision by applying the brakes.

26. Martin Less was killed in the accident on the southbound carriageway of the A1 as he attempted to cross it to get to the Easy Eater service area. ☐

27. Ron Study and Martin Less could have been the two people a motorist said she had seen walking by the side of the A1 South at 23.10. ☐

28. The driver of a passing car said that she was almost in collision with a lorry. ☐

29. Ron Study was asleep in a lay-by when the accident occurred. ☐

30. The Easy Eater service area is located next to the northbound carriageway of the A1 in North Yorkshire. ☐

31. The police car was on a routine patrol of the A1 in North Yorkshire late on Friday night when it came across the scene of the road accident. ☐

Test 3

A robbery was committed on 23 November at 23.10 at a video shop. The robber had a small pistol. The robber made loud gruff noises but said no words. The robber left the shop and got into a car, which was parked outside. The police later found an upturned car in a ditch 25 miles from the shop. It is also known that:

- Steven Tibbs crashed his car at 22.30 on 23 November.
- The cashier was 6 ft 2 in tall.
- Pete Mickson had recently lost his job at the video shop.
- The video shop usually had over £500 in the till.
- The robber was taller than the cashier.
- Pete Mickson was 5 ft 6 in tall.
- Paul Davis drove the getaway car from the video shop.

1. The robber was a man. ☐
2. Steven Tibbs may have been the robber. ☐
3. The cashier reported the robbery to the police. ☐
4. The robber could be a friend of the cashier. ☐
5. Pete Mickson could have been the robber. ☐

At 01.35 on Saturday 9 February a middle-aged man was rushed to All Saints' Hospital with serious face injuries. He is in a critical state in intensive care. Police are looking into the incident which resulted in his injuries. The only other facts known at this stage are:

- There were 14 cm of snow on the pavements in the town.
- The victim was found outside a nightclub.
- The victim's face had been cut by glass.
- Three youths left the nightclub at midnight.
- The victim had been lying outside for over an hour before being taken to hospital.
- The hospital informed the police of the accident.
- The victim had no wallet or identification on him.
- Denis Fraser was the only occupant of the intensive care unit at All Saints' hospital on the morning of Saturday 9 February.

6. The police knew nothing about the accident until the hospital informed them. ☐

7. The victim was Denis Fraser. ☐

8. The victim was drunk. ☐

9. The three youths may have robbed the victim. ☐

10. The victim left the nightclub at 01.15 on Saturday 9 February. ☐

A 13-year-old boy, Gareth Jones, was taken to Downston Police Station on Saturday 11 June under the suspicion of shoplifting in a local superstore. Gareth Jones denies all of the charges made against him. It is also known that:

- Gareth is an orphan.
- The store security officer has a grudge against Gareth because he is the best friend of his son.
- Gareth is not shown on video recordings captured by the store's surveillance cameras.
- Two years ago Gareth was caught stealing police road traffic bollards.
- The store was extremely busy on Saturday 11 June.
- Gareth had not been given a receipt for the goods he had bought.
- Gareth was stopped after he had left the store.

11. The police rang Gareth's mother to tell her where her son was. ☐

12. The store's security officer had a motive for accusing Gareth of shoplifting. ☐

13. This was Gareth's first offence. ☐

14. Gareth had bought some goods at the store. ☐

15. Gareth ran away on leaving the store. ☐

Two masked gunmen held up the only bank in Tuisdale at 10.30 on Wednesday 23 May. They made a successful getaway with over £500,000. The police say that three men are helping them with their enquiries. It is also known that:

- Four people work at the bank.
- Six customers were in the bank at 10.30.
- No shots were fired.
- Ms Grainger left the bank at 10.28 on Wednesday 23 May.
- All the people in the bank were made to lie on the floor face down on their stomachs.
- The police chased the getaway car for 16 km, and then lost it.
- An alarm alerted the police to the hold-up.
- A red Ford Mondeo drove away from the bank at high speed at 10.30 on Wednesday 23 May.

16. One of the gunmen fired a shot to make everyone lie down on the floor. ☐

17. The getaway car was a red Ford Mondeo. ☐

18. The cashier pressed an alarm in the bank, which is connected to the police station. ☐

19. At least six people were lying on the floor in the bank. ☐

20. As a goodwill gesture, Tuisdale's other bank provided emergency access to cash for customers after their ordeal. ☐

All of the students at Risedale High School were sent home early on Tuesday 1 April 2003 due to a bomb scare in the science block. The police were called in after a brown parcel had been left unaccounted for in the physics laboratory. Bomb experts later revealed that it was a hoax. However, the police say that they are treating the matter seriously. So far it is known that:

■ John Dawes, an ex-pupil, was seen in the school grounds on Tuesday 1 April.

■ In the previous week, a group of sixth-form science students had been making minor explosives in the chemistry laboratory.

■ The headteacher had recently made cuts in the science budget.

■ The science staff opposed the recent cuts and had threatened to respond with unreasonable behaviour.

■ Joyce Denver (physics teacher) had bought a birthday present for her son before school on Tuesday 1 April.

■ A recent Inspection Report noted that the school has a high truancy rate.

■ Five pupils have been expelled since the start of the academic year.

21. The brown parcel was the birthday present for Joyce Denver's son. ☐

22. John Dawes had been expelled from Risedale School. ☐

23. The brown parcel could have been intended as an April fool joke. ☐

24. The school has had no other problems with pupils since September 2002. ☐

25. The science staff were free from suspicion. ☐

At 15.25 on Monday 7 August, a 29-year-old man was found dead in his car down a quiet country lane. The police said that the man had died from carbon monoxide poisoning. It is also known that:

- The victim, Giles Clark, was recently appointed sales executive for an electrical firm, Viscox.
- Clark was found gagged with his feet and hands tied.
- Clark had recently lost the company sales worth £250,000.
- A director of Viscox had recently been suspected of fraud.
- Two men of large build were seen walking a Rottweiler down the country lane at 15.10 on Monday 7 August.
- Clark had recently had his car in the garage for a routine service.
- Clara, Clark's wife, had been having an affair with a work colleague, Charles Dence.

26. The two men of large build found Giles Clark's body in the car down the country lane. ☐

27. Clark could have discovered his wife's affair and attempted to commit suicide. ☐

28. Clark was a self-employed sales executive. ☐

29. Clark's car was in need of repair. ☐

30. Viscox had recently suffered financially as a result of lost sales. ☐

31. Clark and a director of Viscox had recently committed fraud against the company. ☐

Test 4

There has been a sudden increase in the occurrence of attempts by confidence tricksters to extract money from elderly people under false pretences. This has caused the police to issue warnings to senior citizens not to let strangers into their homes. So far the police have established the following facts:

- Mr Froode gave £75 to a dark-haired young man posing as a representative of an insurance company.
- Mr Grace paid £80 to a smartly dressed 30-year-old woman who claimed that she was a financial adviser.
- A man who tried to trick 27-year-old Ms Dodds into paying a deposit of £100 towards the cost of a new front door was the driver of a silver grey BMW.
- Over a two-day period a confidence trickster has contacted more than 400 households.
- All of the names and addresses given by the confidence tricksters have been found to be false.

1. The confidence trickster was a transvestite.   ☐

2. Several confidence tricksters, both male and female, were working together.   ☐

3. The confidence tricksters only approached old-age pensioners.   ☐

4. The confidence tricksters may have contacted people first by telephone.   ☐

5. The potential victims all lived in a closely-knit neighbourhood.   ☐

Between 10 and 12 December the police have reported over 120 cases of sharp metal pieces being found in jars of Janesons' mincemeat. The police have evidence that the person responsible is an employee of Janesons. It is also known that:

▪ Janesons has rearranged its management structure and will be making 20 senior employees redundant in January.

▪ Ben Laidet was made redundant on 8 December for incompetent behaviour.

▪ Janesons' closest rival, Bertsons, has been suffering from severe financial losses since Janesons installed new technology in the bottling process, which increased their output.

▪ Engineers recently overhauled the machinery.

▪ Janesons changed its dried fruit suppliers in November.

▪ The mincemeat is put into jars two weeks before going out to the shops.

▪ The seals were unbroken on the contaminated jars.

6. Bertsons will benefit from Janesons' loss of customers. ☐

7. Ben Laidet could have put the metal pieces into the mincemeat. ☐

8. The metal pieces found in the jars of mincemeat may have come from the new suppliers of dried fruit. ☐

9. The contaminated jars of mincemeat were probably bottled between 4 and 7 December. ☐

10. Janesons had recently expanded its output. ☐

A 37-year-old woman was hit and badly injured when a sports car suddenly swerved off the road in the small village of Paddly. She was rushed immediately to Crownsby hospital at 12.45 on Wednesday 3 October, where she is now in a stable condition. A reliable witness said there seemed to be no obvious reason for the car to have swerved so suddenly. The car did not stop and raced out of the village before the police could follow. It is also known that:

- The victim was Jane Scolled.
- Jane worked for a firm of accountants called Sayerston.
- The manager, Mr Sayerston, collected old sports cars.
- Jane had the day off work on Wednesday 3 October.
- Jane had found copies of letters in the office, which indicated fraudulent behaviour by someone in the firm.
- Mr Sayerston plays golf every Wednesday afternoon.
- Jane's father is a renowned barrister in Crownsby.
- At 13.05 a young cyclist was admitted to Crownsby hospital with severe head injuries after being knocked off his bicycle.

11. Jane Scolled was an accountant. ☐

12. While on her lunch break from work Jane Scolled was hit by a car. ☐

13. Just after Jane's accident a car had knocked a young cyclist off his bicycle. ☐

14. Mr Sayerston was afraid of Jane's father. ☐

15. Crownsby hospital dealt with at least two road accident victims on Wednesday 3 October. ☐

On the evening of 3 November a mother and daughter were found dead in their two-bedroom flat in Diswich. Both victims had suffocated and the police are treating the incident as suspicious. It is also known that:

- The victims were Mary Cauld, aged 24 years, and Sarah Cauld, aged 6 years.
- Mary Cauld's father had recently been released from prison.
- Sarah Cauld had been revealed HIV positive on 26 October.
- Gary Davison was Mary Cauld's ex-husband.
- A young man was seen near the flat on 2 November.
- The flat had not been broken into.
- Gary reported the deaths to the police at 6.45 pm on 3 November.
- Mary Cauld was owed £900 by Gary and had threatened to take him to court if he did not pay up soon.

16. Mary Cauld could have killed her own daughter. ☐
17. Gary Davison is a carrier of AIDS. ☐
18. Mary's father was near the flat on 2 November. ☐
19. Sarah Cauld was a healthy child when she died. ☐
20. Gary was the first person to find the two dead bodies. ☐

Two inter-city railway carriages were found ablaze last night (10 March) on a siding near Glundal station. Three elderly men were seen at the station at 19.00 last night and reliable witnesses say that they were all over 6 ft tall and that one of the men had a bad limp. It is also known that:

- The carriages belonged to Southern Trains and were waiting to be repaired.
- Fred Wish is 6 ft 5 in tall and 58 years old.
- Bob Tuck is a retired train driver.
- The railway company made Rod Debbs redundant in January.
- The carriages had been taken out of service because of electrical faults.
- A violent thunderstorm occurred over Glundal on 10 March.
- John Plum is 64 years old and has just left hospital after a knee operation.
- Sixty-one-year-old Dennis White, a former railway worker, is 5 ft 6 in tall.

21. Rod Debbs had a motive for the arson attack. ☐

22. Lightning could have started the fire in the railway carriages. ☐

23. Dennis White was one of the three elderly men seen at the station at 19.00 on the night of the fire. ☐

24. Fred Wish could have been one of the three elderly men seen at the station. ☐

25. Bob Tuck is over 65 years old. ☐

An eminent science professor was found to be in possession of unidentified human body parts, which were stored in his room in the university. His colleagues recall the professor's obsession with his research projects over the past year, and called in the police when the professor's daughter-in-law went missing. It is also known that:

■ The professor had not spoken to his son for two years following an argument.

■ The daughter-in-law visited the professor at the university on a regular basis.

■ The professor had a reputation for being a 'loner' and for working all hours in his study.

■ The professor had once spent several months in a rehabilitation centre.

■ The professor's current research project is concerned with the storage of body organs.

26. The professor was once an alcoholic. ☐

27. The professor enjoyed the company of his daughter-in-law. ☐

28. The professor had been working hard all year on his research projects. ☐

29. The professor could have killed his daughter-in-law for experimental reasons. ☐

30. The son was the only one who called in the police when his wife went missing. ☐

31. The daughter-in-law had gone away following an argument with her husband, the professor's son. ☐

Test 5

Shaun Greene aged 15, was arrested at his mother's home on the Fernbrook Estate on Tuesday 10 June on suspicion of taking a motorcar without the owner's permission on the afternoon of the previous day. He protested his innocence and claimed that he had been at college at the time in question. The following facts are also known:

- The attendance register showed that Shaun was absent from college on both Monday 9 and Tuesday 10 June.
- Shaun's parents are separated and plan to get a divorce.
- When told about the arrest, Shaun's father insisted that Shaun must be innocent because he couldn't drive.
- Shaun's mother admitted that she had allowed him and his elder brother to take her car to some waste ground close to her house.
- The Principal said that Shaun lacks the motivation to succeed, often misbehaves in class and is frequently absent from college.
- When he was younger Shaun had been cautioned for shoplifting.

1. Shaun's parents are separated and he lives with his mother at her home on the Fernbrook Estate. ☐

2. The motorcar in question was taken without the owner's consent on the afternoon of Monday 9 June. ☐

3. Shaun has not previously been in trouble with the law. ☐

4. The father was lying to protect his son when he said that Shaun couldn't drive a car. ☐

5. The college could not corroborate Shaun's explanation of where he was on the afternoon of Tuesday 10 June. ☐

The police are looking for a man aged about 30 who is suspected of committing an assault on a pair of senior citizens outside their home in Chapel Street, Northwell. The alleged assault occurred shortly after 23.00 hours on Thursday 8 July when the couple, Monica and Albert Smart, were returning home from a social evening at their local Community Centre. The following facts are also known:

- Monica and Albert Smith are both aged over 65 and have recently retired.
- An unknown assailant snatched and ran off with Monica's handbag, but Albert refused to hand over his wallet despite being threatened by the thief.
- After the attack, Albert was taken to the A&E Department of City Hospital suffering from severe shock, but was later allowed to return home.
- Bill James aged 32, an unemployed neighbour of the Smarts, was visited by debt collectors on the day of the assault.

6. Theft was the prime motive for the attack on Monica and Albert Smart, a pair of recently retired senior citizens. ☐

7. Albert Smart resisted the thief's attempts to steal his wallet, and was taken to the hospital afterwards to have his injuries treated. ☐

8. Mr and Mrs Smart are long-term residents of Chapel Street, Northwell. ☐

9. Bill James, a neighbour of Mr and Mrs Smart, is currently experiencing financial difficulties. ☐

10. The police are looking for Bill James who is under suspicion for committing the assault on Albert and Monica Smart. ☐

The police report that they have obtained CCTV images of a robbery that took place at a mini-supermarket in a suburb of Littleton. The recordings show that three masked men entered the store in North Road as the duty manager Debra Mooney and her assistants were preparing to close down at about 23.50 BST on Friday 20 April. The following facts are also known:

- Two of the men jumped over the counter and grabbed a quantity of cash from the tills.
- The other man threatened the staff with what appeared to be a kitchen knife.
- None of the staff was injured in the incident but they were badly shaken by the experience.
- Bret Desmond, the brother of one of the assistants, was recently released from prison after serving a sentence for robbery.
- The owner of a nearby hardware store had reported to the police that a set of kitchen knives had been stolen from his shop on the afternoon of Friday 20 April.

11. Bret Desmond, the brother of one of the assistants at the store, has a criminal record. ☐
12. The knife used in the robbery at the mini-supermarket had been stolen from a local hardware shop earlier that day. ☐
13. The raid on the mini-supermarket took place shortly before midnight on the last Friday in April. ☐
14. The CCTV images will enable the police to identify the three men who committed the robbery at the store. ☐
15. The duty manager Debra Mooney and her assistants were subjected to physical violence during the course of the incident. ☐

A young woman, Chantelle Allen aged 20, attacked another woman with the stiletto heel of her shoe after a row broke out between them outside a city centre nightclub at approximately 11.20 pm on Saturday 2 April. Tammy Brown aged 19, was left with a deep two-inch cut on her forehead after the attack. The following facts are also known:

- Gavin More aged 19 was known to have been Chantelle's boyfriend for the past six months.
- Chantelle claimed that Tammy had been sending text messages and photographs of herself to her boyfriend Gavin More.
- Tammy and Gavin used to be in the same class when they were pupils at the local secondary school.
- Gavin and Chantelle had been overheard arguing with each other inside the nightclub shortly before the attack occurred.

16. Tammy has had a crush on Gavin since they were at secondary school together. ☐

17. Gavin and Chantelle had been together at the nightclub on the evening of Saturday 2 April. ☐

18. The heel of a woman's shoe was used to inflict a facial injury on Tammy Brown outside a city centre nightclub. ☐

19. Tammy had been sending Gavin unsolicited text messages and photographs. ☐

20. All three people involved in this incident – Chantelle, Gavin and Tammy – are the same age as each other. ☐

Mrs Hilda Jessop was knocked over by a car on Sutton Road in Forestown at 7.00 pm on the evening of Sunday 8 February. The emergency services were called to the scene of the accident and Mrs Jessop was rushed to the General Hospital, but was later pronounced as being dead on arrival. The following facts are also known:

- Len Peel has been charged at the Magistrates' Court with driving without due care, and causing the death of Mrs Jessop.
- Mrs Jessop was returning home after attending the birthday celebrations of a friend she knew from Church.
- It had rained earlier in the day, but the weather had changed during the afternoon and by early evening the temperatures had unexpectedly fallen to below freezing point.
- The car that Mr Peel was driving when the accident occurred was recently refused an MOT certificate by a local garage because of faulty brakes.
- Local residents have been complaining to the local council about the inadequacy of the street lighting along the stretch of Sutton Road where the fatal accident occurred.

21. The car accident occurred in Sutton Road on the evening of the second Sunday in February. ☐

22. Mrs Jessop was already dead from her injuries by the time the emergency services arrived at the scene of the accident in Sutton Road. ☐

23. The sudden drop in temperature, the road conditions and poor street lighting may have contributed to the car accident in which Mrs Jessop suffered fatal injuries. ☐

24. The car Mr Peel was driving at the time of the accident
   had faulty brakes.   ☐

25. Mrs Jessop was returning home from Church when
   the car accident occurred.   ☐

Fred Knott, a Post Office worker for 30 years, helped to
rescue an elderly man from his car, which was hanging
over the edge of a cliff on the south coast. According to a
statement issued by the local Fire and Rescue Service, it
was only a tree growing at the side of a lay-by that
prevented 69-year-old Mr Ronald Onions, a retired
factory manager, from plummeting 60 feet into the sea
along with his car. The following facts are also known:

■ Fred Knott was on his daily delivery round driving his
  Post Office van along Cliff Road when he spotted Mr
  Onion's car in its precarious position.

■ Mr Onions had recently traded in his old car for a new
  model with automatic gear change and satellite navi-
  gation.

■ The cliff top close to the lay-by has been known locally
  for some years as 'dead man's jump' because of a
  much-publicized suicide that once occurred there.

■ Mr Onions was recently bereaved and had been
  suffering from depression since his wife died.

---

26. Fred Knox was on his routine postal delivery round
   when he spotted the car hanging over the edge of
   the cliff.   ☐

27. If Fred Knox had not arrived at the scene when he
   did, Mr Onions would have plunged down the cliff
   to the sea along with his car.   ☐

28. Unfamiliarity with his new car caused Mr Onions to get into difficulties when pulling into the lay-by on Cliff Road. ☐

29. Mr Onions was a former factory manager and widower. ☐

30. Mr Onions had been depressed since his wife died and had been prescribed anti-depressants by his doctor. ☐

31. If Mr Onions had been attempting to take his own life, and he had succeeded, he would not have been the first to do so at this location. ☐

Answers to verbal logical reasoning tests

Test 1 (page 81)		Test 2 (page 87)		Test 3 (page 94)		Test 4 (page 100)		Test 5 (page 106)	
1	C	1	C	1	C	1	C	1	C
2	C	2	A	2	A	2	C	2	A
3	A	3	B	3	C	3	B	3	B
4	A	4	A	4	A	4	A	4	C
5	B	5	C	5	B	5	C	5	A
6	C	6	C	6	C	6	C	6	A
7	C	7	A	7	A	7	B	7	B
8	A	8	B	8	C	8	A	8	C
9	C	9	A	9	A	9	B	9	A
10	B	10	C	10	B	10	A	10	C
11	C	11	B	11	B	11	C	11	A
12	C	12	C	12	A	12	B	12	C
13	C	13	A	13	B	13	C	13	B
14	B	14	C	14	A	14	C	14	C
15	A	15	C	15	C	15	A	15	B
16	C	16	A	16	B	16	A	16	C
17	B	17	C	17	C	17	C	17	A
18	A	18	B	18	C	18	C	18	A
19	C	19	C	19	A	19	B	19	C
20	B	20	C	20	B	20	C	20	B
21	B	21	C	21	C	21	C	21	A
22	A	22	A	22	C	22	A	22	C
23	B	23	C	23	A	23	B	23	A
24	C	24	A	24	B	24	A	24	C
25	C	25	B	25	C	25	C	25	B
26	B	26	C	26	C	26	C	26	A
27	C	27	A	27	A	27	C	27	B
28	B	28	B	28	B	28	A	28	C
29	A	29	C	29	C	29	A	29	A
30	B	30	C	30	A	30	B	30	C
31	C	31	B	31	C	31	C	31	A

7

Writing tasks and exercises

In the police initial recruitment process there are two occasions when you will be required to demonstrate your written communication skills: **Section 4** of the **Application Form**; and the **written test** at the **assessment centre**. In each case the assessors will be looking critically at the content of what you write, and the writing skills you display – both of which can be related to the core competencies discussed in **Chapter 2**. The **aims** of this chapter, therefore, are to provide you with further guidance on the nature of the writing tasks you will be asked to undertake, and to suggest ways in which you might tackle your preparation for them with a view to increasing your chances of success.

The writing tasks

The writing you will be asked to do in order to complete the application form differs markedly from the written exercise you will be set at the assessment centre. With regard to the former, you will be asked to write answers to some specific questions. In addition, you will be provided with detailed notes to guide you in the way you answer the questions, together with some sample answers.

You can even tell how long your answers should be from the number of lines allocated to the different questions in the application form. However, you are advised to write in the spaces provided because anything outside of those will **not** be marked.

So, in the case of the application form, the writing tasks are known and you have no time limits in which to write the answers. This means that you can write a draft of your answers before you finalize them. Because you have the time to do so, you can also check on the accuracy of your spelling and punctuation. However, the answers you give must be your own work. To ensure that this is the case, you may be questioned at any point in the selection process on the examples you give. In addition, you may be asked to provide the contact details of people who are in a position to verify the accuracy of your accounts of events. So, you must be truthful at all times.

At the assessment centre you will be given two writing exercises, the precise details of which will not be known until the time comes, because part of the test is to see how well you can perform when put on the spot. So, you will have **40 minutes** in which to read the information you are given including the instructions and write your responses – **20 minutes** per task. This means that you will have very little time for drafting and rewriting – you will have to accomplish each piece of writing from beginning to end within the strict time limits of the test.

So, the writing you will be required to do in completing **Section 4** of the application form, and the written test at the assessment centre differ from each other, as do the circumstances under which the writing is undertaken. However, in both cases you will be judged not just on the content of what you write, but also on the quality of your written communication skills. With regard to the latter, you will be expected to:

■ write clearly and concisely – the ability to combine brevity with clarity being an important consideration when you have limited space in which to write your answers, or a short period of time in which to write a report on an incident;

- pay attention to the quality of your handwriting, spelling, punctuation and grammar;
- write in complete sentences, using bullet points only when it is appropriate to do so.

Finally, it is worth remembering that, if the assessors cannot read and understand what you have written, it will be difficult for them to award you the pass grade you need if you are to progress with your application.

Completing Section 4 of the application form

Section 4 of the application form is the point in the selection process when you are asked to begin to demonstrate that you possess the core competencies which are relevant to the role of a police officer. If you are unable to do so your application will not proceed to the next stage. So, completing the application form is not a matter to be taken lightly if you are serious about your intention to pursue a career in the police service.

In this section of the application form you have to provide answers to a total of 10 questions. **Questions 1–4** are broken down into a number of distinct sub-sections. In each case these questions start with a statement about the work of police officers and then ask you to draw upon similar situations from your own experiences to answer a series of numbered questions. As you will see from the questions set out in the box below, in general what you will be expected to do is:

- choose an occasion or a situation from your own recent experience, which matches the criteria you have been given;
- describe specific aspects of that situation;
- give some explanation of your own actions and inner feelings as well as those of other people.

So, it's worth taking a close look at the questions, and thinking hard about them. In particular, you need to reflect on your own experiences in order to select the examples on which you can base your answers. In so doing you should bear in mind the fact that these questions have been designed with an express purpose in mind, ie to give you an opportunity to demonstrate that you possess the core competencies relevant to the role of a police officer. It would be advisable, therefore, for you to refer back to the competency statements given in **Chapter 2**, and to the outcomes of your self-evaluation based upon them. In answering the questions in **Section 4** of the application form, your aim should be to choose examples that enable you to show that you possess the relevant competencies at the required level.

Application Form Section 4 Questions 1–4

Questions 1–4 given below are to be found in **Section 4** of the application form; the number of lines allocated for your answers is given in brackets.

Qn1 It is vitally important that police officers show respect for others, irrespective of their background.

Try to recall an occasion when you have challenged someone's behaviour that was bullying, discriminatory or insensitive. Do not use an example where the other person was simply angry or upset. Their behaviour must have been bullying, discriminatory or insensitive. You will be assessed in this question on how positively you acted, and on how well you understood what had happened.

(i)   Tell us about the situation and about the other person or people involved. (6 lines)

(ii) What did you say, and what did you do? (6 lines)

(iii) **Why do you think the other person behaved as they did?** (4 lines)

(iv) **What would have been the consequences if you had not acted as you did?** (3 lines)

Qn2 Police officers often work in teams and it is important that you are able to work well with others, and are willing to share in the less attractive jobs.

Think of an occasion when it was necessary to work with others to get something done and where you played your part in getting a result. You will be assessed in this question on how well you cooperated with others in completing the task in hand.

(i) **Tell us what had to be done.** (3 lines)

(ii) **How was it that you became involved?** (2 lines)

(iii) **What did you do and what did the others do?** (6 lines)

(iv) **How was it decided how things were going to be done?** (2 lines)

(v) **What did you do to ensure the team were able to get the result they wanted?** (2 lines)

(vi) **What benefit did you see for yourself in what you did (if any)?** (2 lines)

Qn3 Police officers often need to remain calm and act logically and decisively in very difficult circumstances.

Recall an occasion when you have been in a very challenging or difficult situation and had to make a decision that perhaps others disagreed with. You will be assessed in this question on how positively you reacted in the face of difficulty and challenge.

(i) **Tell us about the situation and why you felt it was difficult.** (5 lines)

(ii) **Who disagreed with you and what did they say or do?** (3 lines)

(iii)   **What did you say or do and what did others do?**
(8 lines)

(iv)   **Tell us how this situation made you feel initially.**
(2 lines)

(v)   **How did you feel immediately after the incident?**
(2 lines)

Qn4   **Police officers have to be able to communicate with a wide range of people, both verbally and in writing.**

Try to remember an occasion when you have had to tell a person or a group something that they might have found upsetting or difficult to hear or read. You are being assessed in this question on how you deliver the message and the things you took into account when deciding how to do this.

(i)   **Say who the people involved were and what you had to tell them.** (3 lines)

(ii)   **Why did you think they might find your message upsetting or difficult?** (3 lines)

(iii)   **How did you go about delivering your message? (Tell us what you said, how, where and when.)** (13 lines)

(iv)   **In deciding how to deliver your message, what things did you take into account?** (3 lines)

As you will see from the box below, **Questions 5–10** differ in a number of respects from those discussed above. In addition to being unstructured (ie they are not broken down into sub-sections), they direct the attention to your motivation to become a police officer and your expectations of police work. Clearly, those who devised the questions are interested in establishing why you have applied to join the police service, and whether or not you have thought through the implications of your being successful. If you are going to be in a position to give convincing answers to these questions you will need to give serious thought to them. As part of that process, you will probably need to talk them through with significant others in your life, eg the members of your immediate family and perhaps even close friends.

Application Form Section 4
Questions 5–10

Questions 5–10 given below are also found in **Section 4** of the application form. In each case, an estimate has been given (in brackets) of the number of lines you will be able to write in the spaces provided for your answers.

Qn5 Tell us the reasons why you want to become a police officer. (3 lines)

Qn6 Tell us why you have applied to your chosen police force. (2 lines)

Qn7 Tell us what tasks you expect to be undertaking as a police officer. (4 lines)

Qn8 Tell us what effect you expect being a police officer to have on your social and domestic life. (2 lines)

Qn9 What preparation have you undertaken before making this application to ensure you know what to expect and that you are prepared for the role of police officer? (3 lines)

Qn10 If you have previously applied to be a police officer, Special Constable or Police Community Support Officer, what have you done since your last application to better prepare yourself for the role of police officer? (3 lines)

Now that you know what you will be expected to do, the rest is up to you – as the guidance notes say, 'it must be all your own work'. So, here is a summary of how you might approach this important task:

- Read the notes for guidance given with the application form booklet, paying close attention to the instructions and guidance given.

- Read the sample answers provided in the booklet, taking careful note of the style that has been used. In particular, notice the way in which the first person singular has been used (eg 'I had to make a decision...', and 'I talked to my friends...').

- Make a photocopy of the application form and go through each question carefully, highlighting key words, ie those that tell you exactly what to do.

- Think hard about the examples you might choose as the basis for your answers. Don't settle for the first one that comes into your head – there may be a better alternative.

- Keep in mind that your aim here is to demonstrate that you have the skills, abilities and personal qualities (or 'core competencies') needed to become a police officer.

- Having decided on the example(s) you plan to use, make some notes to help you draft your answers.

- Write out a first draft of your answers.

- Check the drafts to make sure that they are the right length, and that the content fits the purpose, ie that it answers the question.

- Make sure that the quality of your written English meets the criteria listed above (pages 115–16), paying particular attention to your spelling, punctuation and grammar.

- Write the final versions of your answers in the appropriate spaces on the application form, taking care over your handwriting and remembering to keep to the spaces provided.

Assessment centre written test

You will recall from **Chapter 3** that the candidates who are invited to attend an assessment centre are required to undertake a written test. As in the role-play exercises (**Chapter 8**), you will be asked to imagine that you are a Customer Services Officer at a retail and leisure complex ('The Westshire Centre'). In that role you will be required to complete two pieces of writing in the time available (2 × 20 = 40 minutes) and make effective use of the information provided. Remember that the pack gives you information about: the centre (opening hours, access, shops, no-smoking policy, etc); Operations Department; equality policy; code of conduct; and the duties and responsibilities of the Customer Services Officer. You need to be familiar with its contents and to refer to them as and when it is appropriate to do so. The precise details of the writing exercises will be given to you at the time, but the examples given below should help to give you the general idea, and should be used to help you prepare for the 'real thing'.

Example 1

Memorandum

From: Operations Manager
To: Customer Services Officer
Date: 14/02/06

<u>Disabled Car Parking: Letter of Complaint</u>

As a matter of urgency please look into this matter. In your report please indicate how you intend to respond to the letter (attached) I received today from Mr Masters.

Encl. Letter

Letter

M.D. Masters,
Hickory House,
Woodstock,
Perth.
12 February 2006

Dear Sir,
The car parking you provide is awful. I was unable to park by the shops as a Registered Disabled Person. People were in the 2 spaces you provide and they had no disabled stickers. I am very angry at the inconvenience this caused and at the lack of help you provide for people in my position.

Yours faithfully,

David Masters

Example 2

Memorandum

From: Operations Manager
To: Customer Services Officer
Date: 14/06/06

<u>Fire Drill</u>

As a matter of urgency please write me a report on the reasons why yesterday's fire drill failed to meet the standards required by the Fire Regulations. In your report please indicate what steps need to be taken in order to prevent a recurrence of this situation.

Example 3

> ### Memorandum
>
> **From:** Operations Manager
> **To:** Customer Services Officer
> **Date:** 23/12/06
>
> #### Shoplifting
>
> Please write me a short report on this matter including how we might address the increase in shoplifting – a growing cause of serious concern amongst shop owners throughout the Centre.

At first glance all three of the tasks might seem to be pretty straightforward. All you have to do is read the information provided, follow the instructions and write your responses in the form of a report in the time you have been allocated. However, what you need to do at this stage is to look beneath the surface at what you are being told to do and why you are being asked to do it. This involves asking yourself what it is that the assessors are seeking to find out about you by devising these writing exercises, which have to be completed under test conditions at the assessment centre. From what has been said above about answering the questions in **Section 4** of the application form, you should know that the assessors intend to look very closely not just at what you write, but also at how it has been written. In other words, they will be looking for evidence that you have the competencies they are seeking, and that you can use them at the required level. In so doing, they will also be alert to any signals that you give out of 'negative indicators' regarding the way you might act or behave towards others.

So, once again it is worth revisiting those competency statements given in **Chapter 2** to see which of them are appropriate to the writing test at the assessment centre. In so doing, think about how you can apply the competencies you identify to the task in hand, ie writing your replies to the requests set out in the three examples given above. Here are some suggestions as to how you might go about it. First, read each request carefully and ask yourself what it tells you about the person who wrote it, and the problem to which they have drawn your attention. Second, think about what kind of response you would hope/expect to receive if you were the other person, ie try to see the issues from their point of view. Third, think about the actions you could take in order to deal with the problem the person has drawn to your attention. In so doing, try to focus not just on what is practical and feasible, but also on those things that would satisfy your customer's needs.

You should then be in a position to think about how you could write the letter or report, ie not just what you wish to say, but also how best to say it. With regard to the former, you need to say that you acknowledge responsibility for the problem, and to indicate what action you propose to take in order to address it. As far as the latter is concerned, the 'style' you adopt in writing the letter is every bit as important as the accuracy of your use of English. This is where thinking about the needs of your **audience** (the person who will receive your report) is as important as being clear about your **purposes** (the reasons why you are writing the letter).

Because you will be asked to do two pieces of writing under test conditions, you will have no time to waste. You have to approach each one with a clear mind so that you can:

- read the information and the instructions you have been given;
- analyse the causes of the problem and, in so doing, think about it from the point of view of the other people involved – especially the person to whom you have to write a reply;
- work out what you consider to be the best way to deal with the problem – the actions you can and cannot take, and why;

■ decide on the style of writing you need to adopt in order to convey the contents of your reply to good effect.

What you don't need to be doing is worrying about how to set out your report, and whether or not your writing will be full of spelling mistakes and inaccurate punctuation and grammar. You need to get those components of your written communication skills sorted out before you get to the assessment centre. The first item, how to set out your report, is easy to address, but the other matters may be more difficult.

So, let us deal with the easy one first. Take a close look at the sample layout of the outline report set out in **Figure 7.1**. Although there are several acceptable ways of writing such a report, this is one that you can easily adopt for your purposes. What you have to do then is to become so familiar with the way it is structured and written that, when the time comes at the assessment centre, you can concentrate on other things, in other words the content of your report and writing it in such a way that the reader will be able to understand it and it will produce the response you are seeking to achieve.

Once you have become familiar with the layout of such a report, the time has come to put your skills into practice by writing your responses to the two requests given in **Example 1**, **Example 2** and **Example 3**. Write your reports, using the guidance given above. In each case allow yourself **20 minutes** to read the information provided and decide on the content of your response and the style of writing you propose to adopt. Then write the report, remembering to check and proofread it in order to correct any spelling, punctuation or grammatical errors. Once you have completed the reports, ask someone to look at them critically with a view to giving you some constructive feedback. In order to do this they will need to:

■ read the information and instructions on which you have based your reports (**Examples 1–3** above);

REPORT BY: Enter your six-digit candidate number...............

REPORT FOR: Ashley Cheema, Operations Manager.................

Date: ....

PURPOSE OF REPORT: Enter purpose as per instructions...............

Subject matter introduction, ie *'This report concerns the events which occurred...'* (give details of the events).

'As a result of the incident I took the following actions... (give details) *and spoke to the following people...'* (give details, eg Mr X, customer at...).

'With regard to Mr X, I explained that... (give details) *and asked for his views on... being careful to...'* (give details).

'Ms Y was informed about the actions I proposed to take in relation to this incident, especially...' (give details). *'I also explained how these were in line with the Centre's Equal Opportunity Policy, particularly with regard to...'* (give details).

'It should be noted that the following points have come out of this incident:
- *Point one...*
- *Point two...*
- *Point three...*
- *Point four...'* (give details in each case).

'I recommend in order to address points one and two that the following actions be taken...' (give details).

'In order to prevent the reoccurrence of points three and four I recommend that the following procedures be adopted:
- *Procedure one...*
- *Procedure two...'* (give details in each case).

'Please contact me if you would like to discuss any of the matters raised in this report.'

Figure 7.1   Sample layout of a report

- ask themselves if they are satisfied with the content of your reports and, if not, why not;
- think about how you have written your reports, including their structure and your use of English.

Final thoughts

If it emerges from this exercise that you have some serious problems with the standard of your written English you will be well advised to invest some time and effort in an attempt to improve this aspect of your communication skills before you attend an assessment centre. A good starting point for this would be your local tertiary college where the staff should be able to help you to diagnose your strengths and weaknesses, and to advise you on how best to proceed.

8

Role-play exercises

An overview of the role-play exercises used at the assessment centres as part of the police initial recruitment process was given in **Chapter 3**. The **aim** of this chapter is to provide you with further guidance on those role-play exercises, and to suggest ways in which you can begin to prepare yourself for them.

Revisiting the core competencies

The role-play exercises are designed to give you an opportunity to demonstrate to the assessors that you possess the core competencies relevant to the role of a police officer (see **Chapter 2**). Consequently, it might be worth while revisiting those competencies in order to make sure that you are thoroughly familiar with them. To that end, if you have not already undertaken a self-evaluation of the extent to which you 'measure up' against those competencies, now might be a good time to do so. In so doing, remember to crosscheck your own evaluation of the levels of competence you have achieved with someone who knows you well, and whose judgements are reliable.

Time spent reflecting on the judgements you have made about your strengths and weaknesses in relation to the competencies will serve you in good stead, not just in relation to the role-play exercises, but also in connection with the structured interview. It would be helpful to you, therefore, to think about the evidence on which you based your self-evaluations. To that end, can you identify specific events, incidents, or situations you could cite in which your competence was demonstrated? In seeking to do this, you might think about the following questions:

- What happened?
- Where and when did it happen?
- Who else was involved in addition to yourself?
- How did you deal with the situation?
- What were the outcomes of your actions?
- What competencies did you display?

Thinking hard about the competencies, and how you have put them into practice in the past in dealing with problem situations, will help to prepare your mind for both the role-play exercises and the questions you will face in the interview. This is because it will enable you to draw upon your past experiences in order to deal with situations in which you will be expected to 'think on your feet'. In the role-play exercises this could be anything from a shopper who is distressed because she has lost her dog, to an allegation by a member of your staff that a colleague has subjected him to racial abuse. Notice that in both of these cases you will be called upon to deal with a problem – a lost dog and an allegation of racial abuse – as well as the individuals who have ownership of that problem. If you want to do well in the role-play exercises you cannot deal with one and ignore the other.

Role-play exercises – a worked example

For obvious reasons, the 'scenarios' used in the role-play exercises at the assessment centres are changed regularly, and you will be expected to respond positively to whatever situations you are given on the day. Consequently, it is as well at this stage to concentrate on general principles, and how they can be applied in different circumstances. So let's take a look in some detail at an example to see what can be learnt from it.

The situation, which you have to deal with in your role as Customer Care Manager at a large shopping centre, is a woman with a problem – she has lost her dog. She left it tied up outside whilst she did her shopping, and when she returned 10 minutes later it had disappeared. She claims that no one is doing anything to help her to find the animal, and she is clearly very distressed.

You will recall from **Chapter 3** that an actor will play the role of the woman and that you will have five minutes to interact with that role actor. In so doing, you will be expected to show that you understand why the person is feeling so distressed, and that you have a genuine concern to help resolve her problem. Empathy alone will not be good enough, nor will cold-hearted assistance – however practical and common sense that might appear to be. So, in the five minutes of preparation time you will be allowed, you need to think hard about what you can do to deal with both the person and her problem.

However, before you rush off to compile a list of things that you might say and the actions you might take, it is worth while giving some thought to the person with whom you will soon be asked to interact. For example:

- How will they be feeling?
- How is their emotional state likely to affect their behaviour (including the ways in which they might respond to you)?
- How would you feel if you were faced with the same problem?
- How would you like to be treated in such circumstances?

What you are being invited to do by asking these questions of yourself, is to empathize with the other person – an important component of what is known as 'emotional intelligence'.

Given below is a list of possible things you might say and do in this case, which seek to address both the needs of the person and her problem. Think of them as the outcome of a short period of 'brainstorming'. So, they have not been organized into any logical order, nor do they cover all of the options:

- Offer the woman a seat.
- Ask if she would like a drink.
- Establish the facts of the situation by asking relevant questions.
- Start to deal in a practical way with the problem of the lost dog.
- Reassure her that everything will be done to find her dog.
- Organize a search party.
- Inform the security personnel about the loss of the dog.
- Suggest that the security staff speak to other shoppers about the missing dog.
- Offer to arrange her transport home.
- Inform the local police.
- Keep reassuring her that every effort is being made to find her dog.
- Offer to call a relative or a friend on her behalf.

Having studied the list, there are a number of things which you can usefully do. For example, you could begin by adding some suggestions of your own – perhaps as replacements to some that are there already. You could then decide which items in the list are designed to deal with the problem of the lost dog, and which items are intended to address the emotional needs of its owner. You could then put your list of suggestions into an order of priority, starting with the first thing that you are going to say to the person when the role-play begins. Finally, you should try to relate each of the proposed actions to the core competencies as set out in **Chapter 2**. Remember, your aim should be to perform to the required standard in each case, and to avoid displaying any behaviour listed in the competency statements as 'negative indicators'.

You should think of the above as essential advance preparation. But at this stage all you have is a scenario and some ideas for how you might deal with the distressed woman who has lost her dog. What you still have to do is to demonstrate that you can perform to the required standard with regard to the core competencies, ie to put the 'theory' into 'practice'. What you now need to do, therefore, is what actors do when they have studied the script and learnt their lines – rehearse. That means that you need a fellow 'actor' to participate in the role-play situation with you. This is not something that can be entered into lightly – it will only work if both parties take it seriously and have 'done their homework'. In other words, you both need to be familiar with the scenario and understand the roles you are expected to play. You should also try to set up the scene so that it is realistic – if the scenario needs a chair make sure that there is one to hand. Once the role-play begins you should try to:

- get in role immediately – don't be half in and half out;
- take what the other role-player says and does seriously – don't ignore it;
- try to stay calm – however much the other person might try to provoke you and 'throw you off balance';
- remember your plan and try to stick to it – but don't be too inflexible;
- deal with the problem as well as the person;
- try to think ahead – have an idea in your mind about what to say next;
- keep going until the end – don't stop until the time is up (**5 minutes**).

Once the role-play is finished you need to evaluate the experience. Although there are a number of ways in which you can do this, there are two basic questions that need to be addressed, ie how effectively did you manage your interactions with the other person, and how successful were you in dealing with that person's problem(s)? However, it's a good idea to start off the discussion by considering the answers to the longer list of questions given in the box below.

Role-play practice exercises: evaluation questions

Dealing with the situation

Did you take control by dealing with the situation in a positive and decisive manner?

When necessary, were you assertive without being aggressive?

Did you show that you have an alert, enquiring mind?

Dealing with people

Did you display a helpful attitude by being approachable and by offering help where appropriate?

Did you remain calm and constructive when dealing with the situation, even when the other person posed problems?

Did you provide reassurance and support by identifying and responding to people's needs?

Did you manage to prevent your own emotion from affecting the outcome of the situation?

Dealing with information

Did you ask relevant questions?

Did you ask clear, concise questions in order to assess the situation?

Did you check the facts and points of detail?

Did you extract useful information from conflicting sources if that was necessary?

Did you get to the heart of the problem by evaluating the problem and identifying its causes?

Did you make logical decisions in light of the information available to you?

Communication skills

Were you careful of the effects of your communication by taking account of the impact of your words and behaviour on others?

Did you display a friendly and approachable manner?

Were you able to talk at varying levels, depending upon the person or situation?

Were you prepared to listen to information and respond to what was said?

Were you able to summarize pertinent facts?

Were you able to express yourself clearly when speaking?

Both you and your fellow participant in the role-play will have your opinions on these questions, and it's important that both perspectives are considered. For both parties it will also be an exercise in giving and receiving feedback – so listen carefully to what the other person has to say before arriving at any conclusions. You should also put the emphasis on being constructive – both on the things you did well, and what could be done to improve your future performance in role-play situations.

However positive you are, one of the difficulties you will face in this situation is the fact that both of you will be relying on your memories of the interactions which occurred between you. To complicate matters further, you may well have contrary perceptions of what was said and what happened. Consequently, you might consider making an audio or video recording of the role-play exercise, and then reviewing it afterwards as part of the evaluation. The advantage of doing this is that you can replay the tape(s) over and over again if you wish to do so, rather than simply relying on your memory. It is also useful for monitoring your progress over successive role-play practice exercises.

Practice exercises

Now that you have worked through a typical role-play scenario in detail, here are some additional examples for you to practise on as part of your preparation for the role-play exercises.

Example 1

In your role as Customer Care Manager you have to deal with a complaint from an irate librarian that two adolescents are creating a nuisance in the library, which is located within the shopping centre for which you are responsible.

Example 2

In your role as the Customer Care Manager for a shopping centre you have to deal with a male senior citizen who has lost his wallet and pension book and is feeling both angry and distressed.

Example 3

In your role as the Manager of a large warehouse you have to deal with a complaint from one of your staff (a black woman) that she has been the victim of racial abuse from her supervisor.

Example 4

You are the senior waiter on duty in a restaurant and you have to deal with a complaint from a male customer, who appears to have had rather too much to drink, that the food has been poor, and that the service has been shoddy.

Try to work through each of the above examples, following the procedure used in the worked example – the woman and the lost dog. Here is a checklist to remind you of the stages you need to go through in each case:

- Think hard about the person involved – how they will be feeling and how their emotional state is likely to affect their behaviour.
- Generate a list of things you might say and do in order to address both the emotional needs of the person and their problem.
- Relate your proposed actions to the core competencies relevant to the role of a police officer.
- Act out the role-play situation with a fellow actor.
- Evaluate the role-play exercise by addressing the questions given above.

Finally, practise using the following mnemonic (ie a technique for making something easier to memorize) of ISPEAK to structure your participation in the role play-exercises:

Introduce yourself
Summarize the situation
Probe by means of questions the why, where, when, what and how of the situation
Evaluate the events in the light of the Centre's 'Code of Conduct'
Action(s) you will take
Keep it all simple and straightforward

Final thoughts

Although the role-play exercises may seem to be very daunting, the process is designed to be fair. All of the assessors will have been rigorously trained, and in making their assessments they will use a standardized checklist of the competencies which have to be achieved on each exercise. The assessors only assess the candidates' performance on one of the simulation exercises, which means that they are unaware as to how someone has performed on previous exercises. This ensures that a candidate's performance is judged fairly on its merits and that what has happened elsewhere does not prejudice the assessment of their overall performance. Nevertheless, video recordings are made for use in case of an appeal.

From the foregoing discussion it would be easy to assume that you have to be competent in all seven of the core competencies in order to pass. However, this is not the case – all of us have our strengths and weaknesses. So, the role-play exercises aim to assess whether **overall** you have the competencies you will need to perform effectively at the grade of Probationary Constable. Therefore, the assessors will be looking for the inherent skills you possess, as well as your potential for future development.

Finally, when it comes to the role-play exercises at the assessment centre here are a few dos and don'ts:

- **Do** try to be as relaxed as you can – being tense and on edge will detract from your performance, and will be plain for all to see.
- **Do** try to stay calm when speaking to the role actors – even though they may well be trying to get you agitated.
- **Don't** talk too loudly if you can avoid it.
- **Don't** crowd too close into the role actor's 'personal space'.
- **Do** maintain eye contact, but **don't** stare (or 'glare') at the other person.
- **Do** give some thought to your body language, which should be 'saying' to the other person (and to the assessor) that you are fully in control despite the pressure you are under.
- **Do** try to address the emotional needs of the person, and to deal effectively with their problem(s).

9

The interview

In **Chapter 3** we gave a brief introduction to the interview, which is used at the assessment centres as an integral part of the police initial recruitment process. The **aim** of this chapter is to provide you with further information about the use of that interview for the purposes of selecting personnel for the police service, and to suggest ways in which you can prepare yourself for it in order to improve your chances of success.

Selection interviews

The interview is widely used as a method of selecting people for jobs and places on education courses. Employers also use it to assess the suitability of their workers for promotion or further training. Of course, those conducting the interviews are usually armed with additional information about the candidates for selection, including their letters of application, curriculum vitae and references. Nevertheless, much still rests on the final interview in a lot of cases.

However, many employers and others have come to realize that the selection system they had relied upon for so long, with its over-dependence on the interview, was flawed – especially in view of the ways in which the nature of work was changing.

Cultural, social, economic and technological changes mean that the work people do is changing dramatically. Consequently, the skills, abilities and personal attributes they require in order to function effectively in the workplace have also changed. Amongst other things, workers need to be flexible and adaptable, and capable of working with others. The police service is affected by these changes every bit as much as other forms of employment – a fact which is reflected in the competencies now required by police officers (Chapter 2).

One of the ways in which employers have responded to these changes is by recognizing that the interview is a good method for obtaining certain kinds of data about a potential employee, but not for others. Consequently, like the police service now does, they use assessment centres as a means of obtaining a wide range of information about potential recruits prior to making decisions about their suitability for employment. Interviews are still used in that process, but usually as an integral part of the programme at an assessment centre – not as a stand-alone component. As we showed in **Chapter 3**, this will be your experience if you are invited to attend an assessment centre as part of the police initial recruitment process.

Types of selection interview

The first thing to recognize is that there is more than one type of selection interview, and that you need to know where the one you will face at the assessment centre fits into the wider scheme of things. Interviews can be one-to-one, ie where one person interviews an applicant for a job. There are some circumstances in which this might be the most appropriate form of interview to use, eg where someone is seeking to recruit a person with whom they will work closely, and where personal rapport is a crucial consideration. However, in general it is considered to be unsatisfactory as a method of selection because: the interviewer's individual preferences and subjective biases may unduly influence the outcome of the interview; it is impossible for the interviewer to crosscheck their judgements with those of another person.

Consequently, one-to-one interviews can be open to the accusation that the outcomes are not only unreliable, but also potentially unfair to some candidates. This is an important consideration, which organizations like the police service cannot afford to ignore if they wish to be seen as equal opportunities employers. Fairness not only has to be done – it has to be seen to be done.

The alternative to the one-to-one interview is the so-called 'panel interview' at which more than one interviewer is present asking questions. In addition, an observer may also be in attendance in order to ensure that consistent standards are applied, and that all of the candidates receive fair and equal treatment.

Interviews, irrespective of how many interviewers are involved, can be organized in different ways. For example, depending on the degree to which the interactions are structured, three types of interview can be recognized as follows:

▦ **Unstructured interviews** are those in which there is no predetermined set of questions to structure the discussion between the candidate and those asking the questions.

▦ **Semi-structured interviews** are those in which the discussion is structured around a series of key questions to which the candidate is expected to respond. If at any point the interviewers think it appropriate to do so, they ask supplementary questions.

▦ **Structured interviews** are those in which the candidate is asked a predetermined set of questions – usually in strict sequence. Where more than one interviewer is present, this may well involve the individual members of the panel putting the same question to different candidates at the same point in each interview.

The type of interview you should be prepared for if you are invited to an assessment centre falls into the last of these three categories, ie a **structured interview**.

Assessment centre interview

As indicated previously, the interview will last for a maximum of **20 minutes**, which will be structured around **4 questions** you will be invited to answer (4 × 5 = 20 minutes). You will have to wait until the interview itself before you know exactly what the questions are – seeing how you deal with these 'unseen questions' under the pressure of an interview situation is all part of the test. However, you should take comfort from the fact that in many respects the questions will not be dissimilar to those you had to answer in **Section 4** of the application form (**Chapter 7**). So don't be surprised if you are asked to talk about specific situations you have experienced in the past, and to explain how you dealt with them.

You will be allowed up to five minutes to answer each of these four main questions. As the interviewer asks you the question, you will also be given a copy to which you can refer whilst you are speaking. However, once the interviewer has asked you a question, don't expect to be allowed to speak for five minutes without interruption. For example, an interviewer may say something, which acts as a '**prompt**', eg to get you started if you seem to hesitate when asked a question. In addition, the interviewers may ask you a supplementary question (or '**probe**') to encourage you to develop your answer in a particular direction. Some examples of the prompts and probes commonly used by interviewers, and the purposes they are intended to serve, are given in the box below.

Interview prompts and probes

Interviewers use **prompts** as follows:

- If the person being interviewed does not seem to understand the question, eg *'You could start by giving an example from your present job.'*
- If the person being interviewed has given an answer, but seems to be prepared to continue, eg *'Are there any other reasons you can think of?'*
- If the person appears to have finished answering the question, in order to confirm that this is the case, eg *'Have you anything more to add?'*

Interviewers use **probes** as follows:

- To confirm that what the person being interviewed said is what they meant to say, eg *'You seem to be saying that the cause of the problem was outside your control. Is that the case?'*
- To clarify what the person has said, eg *'Could you give some examples of the problems you were facing?'*
- To explain what the person being interviewed has said, eg *'How would you explain the way they reacted to you?'*
- To extend or develop what the person has said, eg *'Could you give more details about the other people involved?'*
- To make links with things that the person had said earlier in the interview, eg *'How did this compare with the first situation you described?'*

You should note that the interview is also an opportunity for the interviewers to seek clarification of anything that has arisen out of the scrutiny of your application thus far. So, don't be surprised if in addition to the main questions you are asked about other matters relevant to your application. Hence, it is a good idea to make a photocopy of your application form and to study it before you arrive at the assessment centre. In this way you should be familiar with its contents, making it unlikely that you will be 'caught out' if and when you are questioned about them in your interview.

In addition to asking you questions, the interviewers will be doing two things in order to assess your performance, ie they will be listening to what you say and observing your non-verbal behaviour or 'body language'. With regard to the latter, the way you are viewed by those interviewing you will be as important as the things you have to say – they will be an integral part of your assessment. So what are the essential points of body language you should be seeking to project during your interview? A checklist of the most important things to bear in mind is given in the box below.

Body language checklist

- Enter the room confidently, ie don't sidle in as if you would prefer not to be there.
- Sit well back on the seat, ie try to look as if you are comfortable with the fact that you will be there for some time.
- Don't perch on the edge of the seat, ie don't look as if you are anxious to leave at the first opportunity.
- Sit with both feet on the floor and lean slightly forward towards the interviewers.
- Don't slump in your seat with your head bowed towards the floor.
- Make eye contact with all of the interviewers. When answering a question concentrate your attention mainly on the person who asked it – but don't neglect the others.
- When making eye contact with the interviewers try to be aware of the messages they are communicating non-verbally to you.
- Be prepared to smile if the opportunity presents itself, eg if you recall something amusing that happened in a situation you have been asked to describe.

- Don't fold your arms or cross your legs – such actions may be taken as a signal that you are on the defensive.
- Relax your hands in your lap and try to keep them still – don't fidget or put them in your pockets.
- Remember to monitor your body language during the course of the interview and to change it if necessary – it is all too easy to forget about it under the pressure of answering all those questions.

So much for your body language, but what about the way in which you should respond to the interviewers' questions? Clearly, you will have to organize the content of what you say in order to deal with specific questions you have been asked. However, there are certain guidelines for answering any question in an interview if you wish to make a positive impact on those who are assessing your performance. A list of the most important things to bear in mind is given in the box below.

Responding to interview questions

- Listen carefully to the questions, and answer them as fully as you can.
- Don't ramble on by volunteering irrelevant information. Stop talking once you think that you have said all that you need to say – if the interviewers want you to say more they will ask you supplementary questions (see what was said above about 'prompts' and 'probes').
- Avoid very short, one-word answers unless it is in response to a specific question, which asks for an answer of that kind.
- Be prepared to support what you say with specific examples drawn from your own experience.
- If you need time to think before answering a question, be prepared to pause for a moment – it shows that you are giving careful consideration to how best to answer.

- ▪ Ask for clarification if you don't understand what the interviewer is asking you – it's far better to do that than to launch into answering a question you have only half understood.
- ▪ Try to be as open and honest as you can in answering the questions – even to the extent of admitting that there are things that you don't know. Above all, don't change the facts to suit your case.
- ▪ Remember the competencies relevant to the role of a police officer (**Chapter 2**), and use the outcomes of your self-evaluation in framing your answers to the questions.

Interview practice exercises

You will be asked **four** questions relating to the core competencies set out in Chapter 2, and you will be allowed a maximum of five minutes per question to answer them. If you have followed the advice given elsewhere in this book, the work you have done thus far should serve you in good stead when it comes to preparing for the interview. For example, if you completed the self-evaluation exercise we suggested in **Chapter 2** you should have become thoroughly familiar with the core competencies required by police officers. The four main questions applicants are asked in the interview are just another way of seeking evidence that they possess those competencies at the required level – so it is worth going back over them again to refresh you memory. Similarly, if you gave serious thought to answering the questions in Section 4 of the application form, you should be able to identify situations from your own experience, to describe those situations and explain how you dealt with them. The difference here is that you do it orally, rather than in writing, and you have to do it on the spot in the presence of those asking you the questions. Finally, the preparatory work you should have done for the role-play exercises should have given you some insights into the kinds of problem situations you might be asked to talk about in your interview. In addition, if you have practised for those role-play exercises you should have become accustomed to interacting with other people, and in doing so 'thinking on your feet' – skills that will come in useful in the interview. Nevertheless, there are some exercises which you can usefully do in preparation for the interview.

A good starting point is to practise thinking through how you can structure your answer to a question bearing in mind that the interviewers are likely to ask you some supplementary questions during the course of the interview. To give you the idea let's take two questions to see how you can break them down in order to structure how you might go about answering them.

Question 1

'Can you give an account of an occasion when a person was treated badly in your presence because of their background (eg their age, ethnicity, gender or religion), and explain how you behaved in that situation.'

This is clearly a question which focuses on the core competency 'Respect for Race and Diversity' – but not to the exclusion of the other competencies. The first thing you have to do is to identify the example on which you are going to base your answer to the question. Having done that, work your way through the following sub-questions writing down a short answer to each of them:

- How did the situation arise – what were the circumstances that led to it?
- What actions did you take and why?
- What were the results of your actions?
- If you had not acted as you did what might have happened?
- What did you learn from the experience?
- How have you put that learning into practice?

Question 2

'Describe an occasion when you accomplished a task through working with other people as part of a team.'

This is obviously a question that focuses on the core competency 'Team working' – but not to the exclusion of the other competencies. Once again, you should start by identifying the example on which you are going to base your answer to the question. Then, work your way through the following sub-questions writing down a short answer to each of them:

- How did the situation arise – what were the circumstances?
- What was it that you were trying to accomplish – what was the task?
- Who else was involved?
- What approach did you adopt to accomplishing the task?
- What difficulties did you encounter?
- What actions did you take to resolve those difficulties?
- What were the results of your actions?
- If you had not acted as you did what might have happened?
- What did you learn from the experience?

Notice that what you have done in each case is to produce the information on which you can base your answer as well as a logical sequence in which you can present it. What you need to do is remember the order in which you intend to deal with that information so that you don't have to worry too much about the detail – because you should be able to recall that as and when the need arises. However, if there are any points of detail which are of particular significance, you should make sure that you have committed them to memory. You might find it helpful in these circumstances to use the following mnemonic as a memory aid: **CAR** ie Circumstances, Actions and Results – remembering with the last one to point out how the results might have been different had you not acted as and when you did. Bear in mind that you will only have about five minutes to answer the question; about a minute and half for each of the sub-sections if you are following the **CAR** mnemonic.

When you have done that you could rehearse answering the questions in your mind, or out loud in front of a mirror. Alternatively, get someone to act as your interviewer and ask you to answer one of the two questions given above. In so doing, try to replicate the formality of an interview situation in terms of the arrangement of the furniture, where you both sit, and the way in which you greet each other at the outset, for example. In other words try to get into role as you were invited to do when you practised for the role-play exercises in **Chapter 8**.

Afterwards, review your performance using the guidelines given above for body language and responding to interview questions. Repeat the process with the second question. If you have the facilities to do so, audio or video record your interactions with your interviewer and use the recording for the purposes of evaluation. Make sure that you put the emphasis on the positive aspects of your performance, ie what you did well and the things that you can work on in order to improve next time.

Having done that, now work out how you would answer the questions given in the box below. In doing so, try to apply the method used in connection with the practice exercises based on **Question 1** and **Question 2** given above. Once you have done that get someone to ask you the questions as if you were in an interview. Take it one question at a time, but don't just repeat the process. Instead of just 'going through the motions', give yourself something specific to work on each time with a view to improving your performance. For example, as a result of the feedback you have been given or from your own self-evaluation, it might be that you decide to concentrate on how you start your answer, or the way you bring it to a conclusion.

Practice questions

- Can you describe a situation in which your work was criticized, and explain how you responded to that criticism?
- Can you explain how you cope with difficult routine tasks (or people) at work?
- Can you give an account of a difficult situation or problem, which you helped to resolve?
- What have you done/are doing to develop your potential?
- What have you done to prepare yourself for the assessment centre?

Final thoughts

The interviewers will signal when the interview is finished. At that point stand up and prepare to leave, eg by collecting your possessions. However, if you remember something that would strengthen any of your answers, and you have time left you can go back to the question and add to what you said earlier – so long as it is within your allocated 20 minutes. Don't expect the interviewers to say anything about your performance or the likely outcome of the interview. However, if they offer you their hands, shake them before you go – but don't be lulled by the official end to the interview into making any unguarded comments. So, simply thank them for their time and attention and then make a calm and unhurried exit from the room.

10

Job-related fitness test

During the course of their duties, police officers are often required to perform tasks which are physically demanding. It is essential, therefore, that they possess a standard of physical fitness which enables them to perform these tasks professionally and without risk of injury. It is for this reason that minimum standards of physical fitness have been defined which must be achieved by candidates wishing to join the police service. Detailed information about the test and how to prepare for it are given in a booklet entitled 'Job Related Fitness Test For Police Recruitment', which is included in the application pack. The **aim** of this chapter is to provide you with a brief introduction to the tests and to the content of that booklet. Our advice is that if you want to improve your chances of success in the fitness test you should obtain that booklet, read it carefully and follow the advice you are given.

The tests

■ First, this test is one which you must pass before your application can proceed further – it does not matter how well you have done in the other assessment tests.

- To pass the physical fitness test overall you must achieve a satisfactory standard in both components.
- If you fail the fitness test you will be allowed to retake it, and if you fail the test again you will be given one more chance to take it.
- If you fail three consecutive fitness tests your application will be withdrawn, and you will not be eligible to reapply for 12 months.
- So, take it seriously and prepare and train properly for it – and if you do there is no reason why you should fail.
- If your application is successful, your fitness will be assessed regularly during your training. Failure to pass the test at that stage will lead to your being dismissed from the service.

It is essential, therefore, that you establish and maintain your level of fitness to the required standard. The tests you are required to take have been devised to measure the fitness qualities that police officers need to perform the physical tasks that are an integral part of their duties. The tests provide evidence of your endurance fitness and your dynamic strength. The tests run one after another and a minimum standard must be achieved on each of them. On completion of the tests, individual scores are accumulated and a pass or fail mark is formulated.

Test 1: endurance fitness

Police officers are sometimes required to perform prolonged activities that demand stamina, such as chasing people on foot, climbing stairs and attending to public order duties. The ability to perform activities such as these is based on your level of what is known as 'endurance fitness', ie your capacity to continue with prolonged physical activity. This reflects how efficiently your heart and lungs are working – something that is required in any activity that causes you to get out of breath. This kind of fitness is also important in police officers because if they become physically tired it is hard for them to stay mentally alert and to be able to respond appropriately to difficult (and at times dangerous) situations as and when they occur.

Your endurance fitness will be tested by your running to and fro along a 15-metre track and placing your leading foot on each end line in time with a series of audio bleeps. The test is progressive in that the timing of the bleeps starts off slowly but becomes faster, making it more difficult for you to keep up with the required speed. You will be expected to keep running until you can no longer keep up with the set pace. You will need to reach a minimum of one shuttle at level 5.4 to pass this part of the fitness test.

Test 2: dynamic strength

Police officers are sometimes required to restrain and arrest individuals who are struggling and/or fighting. This can involve pushing, pulling and grappling over a period of time. The ability to perform such activities requires dynamic strength of the upper body. Possessing high levels of such strength will also lessen your chances of physical injury.

The test involves the use of a machine called a 'Dyno' on which you will be required to perform five seated chest pushes (with three seconds of recovery between each push) and five seated back pulls (again with three seconds of recovery between each pull). You will be allowed to perform three warm-up pushes and pulls before your scores are recorded. The average force of the sum of five pushes, and the average force of the sum of five pulls will be measured. The lower score recorded (ie for either the push or the pull) will determine the overall level awarded for the dynamic strength test. In order to pass you will need to achieve an average score of 34 kilograms to pass on the push test and 35 kilograms on the pull test.

How to improve your test scores

The booklet will provide you with detailed guidance on how you can improve your levels of fitness so that you can improve your performance on both these tests. However, owing to the scheduling of the recruitment process, you should expect to receive very little notice of your test dates. Consequently, you are strongly advised to start training for your fitness test as soon as possible. Familiarization courses, which allow you to practise the job-related fitness tests, are held regularly by police forces throughout England and Wales. You are advised to contact the nearest recruitment centre if you would like to obtain further information about these familiarization courses or make any query regarding the job-related fitness test.

11

Some final thoughts

The **aim** of this concluding chapter is to offer you some final words of advice with a view to furthering your preparation for the police initial selection system. In so doing, attention will be drawn to the importance of aspects of your personal development which, in the interest of attending to the specific requirements of particular tests, have been understated in earlier chapters.

Developing your reading skills

At a number of points in this book you have been strongly advised to read the instructions and questions carefully to make sure that you understand them, and have assimilated all the relevant written information before you start to respond. This is because the effectiveness of your reading skills will affect your ability to:

- answer the questions in Section 4 of the application form;
- solve problems in the verbal logical reasoning test;
- respond appropriately to the instructions in the written exercises;
- deal adequately with situations in the role-play activities;
- make effective use of the information provided in 'The Westshire Centre' 'Welcome Pack'.

In each case, if you misread the instructions, or fail to recognize the significance of information you have been given, you cannot hope to give correct answers or deal appropriately with a situation. You should also bear in mind that in all of the above cases, with the exception of the application form, you will be required to use your reading skills under the pressure of test conditions, ie when you know you are being tested, and when you have a limited time to read the text, make decisions and respond to the instructions. The problem is particularly acute in the verbal logical reasoning test – as you may well have found already from the practice tests (**Chapter 6**). So, given their all-round importance, it may be worth your while to put some effort into polishing up your reading skills.

Unfortunately, the trouble with our reading skills is that once we have acquired them we have a tendency to take them for granted. We seem to think that, like riding a bike, once you have learnt them you never forget. In fact, what many people don't realize is that over the years they have developed a wide range of reading skills, which they deploy without thinking about it. What skilled readers do is to vary the methods they use according to two things – **what** they are reading and **why** they are reading it. Now think about how this principle might apply to your own reading. You can do that by working through the examples given in the box below.

Think carefully about how you read each of the following:

- a novel you have taken with you on holiday;
- a contract you have been asked to sign;
- a newspaper to find out about your favourite team;
- the instructions which tell you how to operate a new piece of hi-fi equipment, or how to assemble an item of flat-pack furniture;
- the *Yellow Pages* to find a telephone number.

What that exercise should have demonstrated to you is that there is more to being a skilled reader than you perhaps realized, and that with a bit of thought and effort you can make the reading skills you use more explicit. Having done that, you can set about developing them with a view to using them to your advantage, ie to help you perform better in the police initial recruitment tests. You can start that process by reading and making use of the reading skills set out in the box.

Tips for developing your reading skills

- Use the contents page, eg of a magazine, book or report, to get a quick impression of the information it contains, and to find out how it is structured.
- Note the titles of chapters, and the headings given to sections, sub-headings and paragraphs, which summarize for you what the text is about.
- Skim read the text, ie read it quickly and selectively to pick out the key points or ideas.
- Scan the text, ie look quickly at all parts of the text in order to get an overall impression of what it is about – don't get 'bogged down' in the detail.
- Ask yourself questions, eg 'What is this all about?' 'Does it make sense? 'Do I need to know this?'
- Underline or highlight words, phrases and sentences, eg in order to identify key points in an argument, or to distinguish facts from opinions.
- Annotate the text, eg by inserting headings and sub-headings, listing key points and writing comments in the margin.
- Draw arrows, eg to link points which you have highlighted, or underlined elsewhere in the text or to connect parts of the text with a diagram or table of statistics.
- Write summaries of key points or arguments, eg in a chapter of a book or section in a report.
- Work out the meaning of words and terms that you do not understand from the context in which they are used.

Over a relatively short period of time, training yourself to use the skills listed above should help you to become a more effective reader. In so doing, you will enhance your reading skills, which in turn should increase your chances of interpreting instructions correctly and responding appropriately – even under the pressure of an assessment centre. However, as with physical fitness, don't leave it too late to start getting your reading skills into shape. It may take longer than you think.

Developing your listening skills

As with reading skills, at a number of points in this book you have been advised to listen carefully to what people are saying to you in order to understand what has been said. This is because the effectiveness of your listening skills will affect your ability to:

■ respond properly to the verbal instructions you will be given in the psychometric tests and the written exercises;
■ interact appropriately with the actors in the role-play activities;
■ answer questions correctly in the interview.

In each case, if you misread what is said, or fail to recognize the significance of information you have been given orally, you cannot hope to deal with the situation to the best of your ability. You should also bear in mind that in all of the above cases, you will be required to use your listening skills under the pressure of being tested at the assessment centre. So, given their ability to have a profound effect on your performance, it is undoubtedly worth your while to develop your listening skills – however fine-tuned you think they are already.

If you think about it, it is obvious that effective communication is a two-way process. In other words, you are not just the encoder and transmitter of messages to other people – you are also the target for their communications. Consequently, you have to pay attention if you are to receive and correctly decode the various messages they are sending out to you. So, because it is a two-way street, communication is not just about talking to people. It's also about listening to (and looking at) them as well, if you wish to interpret correctly what it is that they are trying to say to you. However, because modern society is so culturally diverse, there is a good chance that you will not even be talking a 'common language'. This is despite the prevalence in this country of the use of English – though not necessarily as their first language for many people. Hence, in order to be able to communicate effectively, we have to be able to do so in contexts which are culturally diverse. In order to do this we need to take into account the ways in which differences, eg in age, education, ethnicity, gender, nationality and social background, can lead to variations in the following:

- tone of voice and patterns of stress by which the flow of information is managed, meaning is clarified and emotions are expressed;
- patterns of 'taking turns' in conversation;
- ways of expressing agreement and disagreement, eg when someone says 'Yes' does it mean 'I've heard you' or 'I agree with you'?
- codes and conventions used for signalling politeness;
- ways of structuring arguments and information;
- how emotions are expressed – including the extent to which it is considered appropriate to express emotions in particular situations.

It is easy to see, therefore, why misunderstandings can arise when two people from different 'speech communities' try to talk to each other, especially if each person interprets what the other is saying from the perspective of their own culture. If you are not careful, such a situation could occur at the assessment centre in the role-play exercises. One of the starting points for avoiding potential breakdowns in communication is to do some work on your listening (and related observational) skills. Some suggestions for doing that are given in the box below.

Tips for developing your listening skills

- When you are in a garden, in a park, out in the country or even in a crowded room or street, make a mental note of the different things you can hear. Then close your eyes and concentrate on listening for a few moments. What can you now hear that you hadn't noted before?
- In a situation in which you are able to do so (eg a one-to-one conversation or a meeting), practise giving the speaker your full attention – if you allow yourself to be distracted it will affect your listening. Remember that 'your full attention' means listening carefully to what they are saying, and watching them closely.
- In such situations, practise maintaining your concentration – avoid 'switching off' if you disagree with what is being said or you think you already know what is coming next.
- Try to give positive feedback to the speaker to indicate that you are listening – explore both the verbal (eg '*I agree with what you're suggesting*') and the non-verbal (eg a nod of the head).
- Check the information that you have heard with the speaker, eg '*Am I right in understanding that ...?*' In so doing, gauge their reactions (both verbal and non-verbal) to what you have said.
- At an appropriate point, summarize what you see as being the main points the speaker has made.
- Record a broadcast discussion (radio or television) and use it to practise your listening skills. For example, concentrate your attention on the differences in opinions as expressed by different speakers, or in the case of a video recording focus your attention on the speakers' body language.

Time spent on activities such as those listed above should help to sensitize you to the importance of your listening (and related observation) skills. Developing these skills should enhance your ability to interpret correctly what others are saying, and to respond appropriately to them in both the role-play exercises and the interview. However, as with the other skills you are seeking to develop, it will take time and effort on your part – so don't put off making a start for too long.

Emotional intelligence

If you look again at the core competencies and think carefully about the various forms of assessment you will be subjected to as part of the selection process – especially at the assessment centre – it is evident that the police service is looking for recruits who possess certain personal qualities and attributes. The people they select have to be physically fit and mentally able – they must also be capable of acting and behaving in an appropriate manner in situations they encounter during the course of their duties. Hence, the police service is looking for people who are aware of the impact they are having on others, can keep their inner feelings under control when it is appropriate to do so, who can empathize with the situation other people find themselves in, who are motivated to do their duty, and have the social skills which enable them to relate to, and influence others. The name given to this combination of personal attributes is 'emotional intelligence'.

It is generally recognized that emotional intelligence is made up of five components or areas of competence:

- **self-awareness**, ie knowing yourself and what your inner feelings are telling you;
- **self-regulation**, ie having the ability to manage and control your own inner emotions – even under the severest pressure;

- **motivation,** ie channelling your emotions to enable you to do your duty and to achieve your goals;
- **empathy,** ie recognizing and 'reading' the inner feelings of others, and responding appropriately to them in all cases;
- **social skills,** ie relating to, and influencing the behaviour and actions of others.

However, these components are all connected to each other in complex ways – the ability to perform effectively in any one being related to how capable a person is in one or more of the others. Thus, handling your feelings in such a way that you behave appropriately (self-regulation) is built on knowledge of your inner self (self-awareness). Similarly, anyone who is in touch with and understands their own emotions (self-awareness) is likely to be able to read the feelings of other people (empathy). Being able to relate appropriately to others (social skills) is a function of all the others. Finally, without self-knowledge, that which powers our achievements (our motivation) will not come into play.

Like your reading skills, therefore, the competencies which make up emotional intelligence underpin your ability to perform effectively in the selection process.

Final advice

Given below are some final words of advice of a general nature – advice which goes beyond that given in the individual chapters, which by necessity focused on particular aspects of the selection process:

- Start your preparation for the recruitment process as early as you can – don't leave it until it is too late. In this respect, the advice you were given concerning the build-up of your physical fitness applies equally to other aspects of your personal development – working on your reading skills, practising psychometric tests, improving your writing skills and developing your role-play and interview techniques all take time.

■ The fact that in order to pass you have to reach a satisfactory standard on all of the assessment tasks means that you cannot afford to neglect any one of them – you have to work on developing an 'all-round game' in which you have no major weaknesses.

■ Make sure that you are fully familiar with the competencies relevant to the role of a police officer, eg by using the competency statements to audit your strengths and weaknesses.

■ Use the outcomes of that self-evaluation to draw up a personal development action plan, which seeks to build on your strengths and addresses your weaknesses.

■ In drawing up an action plan it always helps to be clear about what you are trying to achieve (your goals), and to set yourself some realistic targets. With the latter, lay down achievable deadlines.

■ When it comes to implementing your action plan, don't try to do everything in a rush, and all at once. It may be better at times to concentrate your attention on one or two things to the exclusion of others, eg on developing your number skills, or working on your writing skills. Much will depend on such matters as how well you manage your time, and how you learn best.

■ Keep a record (perhaps in the form of a diary or a log) of what you have done and what you think you have learnt. Use it from time to time to review your progress, eg by comparing the goals and targets in your action plan with what you think you have achieved. Adjust your plans in the light of the outcomes.

■ If your self-evaluation suggests that you have weaknesses in certain areas, which you cannot address by yourself, seek guidance from the appropriate places. Your local tertiary college is an obvious starting point, but help is also available from other sources, which can be accessed via the web.

■ Enlist the support of others – you are going to need people who are willing to help you in a variety of ways, eg you may be the kind of person who needs someone to help you to get fit by going with you to the gym. Above all, you are going to need at least one 'critical friend' – someone who is prepared to give you some honest feedback about yourself at times and to do it in such a way that you remain friends. It would also help if that person would agree to help you with the practice exercises, especially the role-play and the interview.

Whilst we urge you to take your preparation seriously, we hope that you enjoy the process of following the guidance offered in this book, and that you take some satisfaction from furthering your own development. Good luck with the selection process.

Further Reading from Kogan Page

Advanced IQ Tests
ISBN 978 0 7494 5232 2
The Advanced Numeracy Test Workbook
ISBN 978 0 7494 5406 7
Aptitude, Personality & Motivation Tests
ISBN 978 0 7494 5651 1
The Aptitude Test Workbook
ISBN 978 0 7494 5237 7
A-Z of Careers & Jobs
ISBN 978 0 7494 5510 1
Careers After the Armed Forces
ISBN 978 0 7494 5530 9
Career, Aptitude & Selection Tests
ISBN 978 0 7494 5695 5
Graduate Psychometric Test Workbook
ISBN 978 0 7494 5405 0
Great Answers to Tough Interview Questions
ISBN 978 0 7494 5196 7
How to Master the BMAT
ISBN 978 0 7494 5461 6

How to Master Nursing Calculations
ISBN 978 0 7494 5162 2
How to Master Psychometric Tests
ISBN 978 0 7494 5165 3
How to Pass Advanced Aptitude Tests
ISBN 978 0 7494 5236 0
How to Pass Advanced Numeracy Tests
ISBN 978 0 7494 5229 2
How to Pass Advanced Verbal Reasoning Tests
ISBN 978 0 7494 4969 8
How to Pass the Civil Service Qualifying Tests
ISBN 978 0 7494 4853 0
How to Pass Data Interpretation Tests
ISBN 978 0 7494 4970 4
How to Pass Diagrammatic Reasoning Tests
ISBN 978 0 7494 4971 1
How to Pass the GMAT
ISBN 978 0 7494 4459 4
How to Pass Graduate Psychometric Tests
ISBN 978 0 7494 4852 3
How to Pass the Police Selection System
ISBN 978 0 7494 5712 9
How to Pass Numeracy Tests
ISBN 978 0 7494 5706 8
How to Pass Numerical Reasoning Tests
ISBN 978 0 7494 4796 0
How to Pass Professional Level Psychometric Tests
ISBN 978 0 7494 4207 1
How to Pass the QTS Numeracy Skills Test
ISBN 978 0 7494 5460 9
How to Pass Selection Tests
ISBN 978 0 7494 5693 1
How to Pass Technical Selection Tests
ISBN 978 0 7494 4375 7

How to Pass the UKCAT
ISBN 978 0 7494 5333 6
How to Pass the UK's National Firefighter Selection Process
ISBN 978 0 7494 5161 5
How to Pass Verbal Reasoning Tests
ISBN 978 0 7494 5696 2
How to Succeed at an Assessment Centre
ISBN 978 0 7494 5688 7
IQ and Aptitude Tests
ISBN 978 0 7494 4931 5
IQ and Personality Tests
ISBN 978 0 7494 4954 4
IQ and Psychometric Tests
ISBN 978 0 7494 5106 6
IQ and Psychometric Test Workbook
ISBN 978 0 7494 4378 8
IQ Testing
ISBN 978 0 7494 5642 9
The Numeracy Test Workbook
ISBN 978 0 7494 4045 9
Preparing the Perfect Job Application
ISBN 978 0 7494 5653 5
Preparing the Perfect CV
ISBN 978 0 7494 5654 2
Readymade CVs
ISBN 978 0 7494 5323 7
Readymade Job Search Letters
ISBN 978 0 7494 5322 0
Succeed at IQ Tests
ISBN 978 0 7494 5228 5
Successful Interview Skills
ISBN 978 0 7494 5652 8
Test and Assess Your Brain Quotient
ISBN 978 0 7494 5416 6

Test and Assess Your IQ
ISBN 978 0 7494 5234 6
Test Your EQ
ISBN 978 0 7494 5535 4
Test Your IQ
ISBN 978 0 7494 5677 1
Test Your Numerical Aptitude
ISBN 978 0 7494 5064 9
Test Your Own Aptitude
ISBN 978 0 7494 3887 6
Ultimate Aptitude Tests
ISBN 978 0 7494 5267 4
Ultimate Cover Letters
ISBN 978 0 7494 5328 2
Ultimate CV
ISBN 978 0 7494 5327 5
Ultimate Interview
ISBN 978 0 7494 5387 9
Ultimate IQ Tests
ISBN 978 0 7494 5309 1
Ultimate Job Search
ISBN 978 0 7494 5388 6
Ultimate Psychometric Tests
ISBN 978 0 7494 5308 4
Verbal Reasoning Test Workbook
ISBN 978 0 7494 5150 9

Sign up to receive regular e-mail updates on Kogan Page books at **www.koganpage.com/signup.aspx** and visit our website: **www.koganpage.com**